The
GROUPWORK
MANUAL

Andy Hickson

Speechmark

Speechmark Publishing Ltd
Telford Road • Bicester • Oxon OX26 4LQ • UK

Published by

Speechmark Publishing Ltd, Telford Road, Bicester, Oxon OX26 4LQ, United Kingdom
www.speechmark.net

© A Hickson, 1997
Reprinted 2000, 2002

002-2615/Printed in the United Kingdom/1030

British Library Cataloguing in Publication Data
Hickson, Andy
  The groupwork manual
  1. Social group work
  I. Title
  361.4

ISBN 0 86388 408 3

(Previously published by Winslow Press Ltd under ISBN 0 86388 178 5)

Contents

To you

from me

from you

to me

Full of inspiration and creativity

I love you all

Foreword

I can give a heartfelt endorsement for the *Groupwork Manual*. It is addressed to people like myself, those who are teachers, trainers or convenors of meetings, and yet who know little or nothing about the dynamics of groupwork. We work in a vacuum. We focus on the topic which we put before our group, but we lack the resources for placing the topic within the context of the group. In my own case, I practise in a classic didactic teaching mode, ie. I impart information from myself (teacher) to my audience (students). Though the lessons might include heated arguments and debate, they are not groupwork. They are no more groupwork than *Question Time* on UK TV. I am incapable of harnessing the energy of the group to assist in my endeavour. Why? Because I have no idea about the dynamics of groupwork.

Andy Hickson's *Groupwork Manual* allows me to expand my skills. It gives me a sound introduction as to what constitutes a group and it provides me with a practical guide, in a wonderful series of exercises ranging from name games to rituals, as to how to harness the dynamic of the group. It is a brilliantly written manual, concise and comprehensive, theoretical and practical, a treasure-trove of information and fun to read. It could only be written by a true expert and comes from Andy's years of experience as an outstanding groupwork practitioner. In addition to amateurs like myself, it is also of major importance to those who specialise in groupwork. We are all indebted to Andy for distilling his knowledge and offering it to us with such skill, grace and clarity.

Dr Robert Silman, 1997

Acknowledgements

Many people have helped in the writing of this book, particularly the contributors who wrote stories and anecdotes for me to include. Thank you Frances Babbage, Clive Barker, Franc Chamberlain, Glenn Dallas, Bill Davis, Cath Davis, Frances Davis, David Dean, Chloe Gerhardt, Myfanwy Harrington, Cyril Ives, Sue Emmy Jennings, Robert Landy, Rachael Perry and Robert Silman. You all made the book. I would also like to thank Stephanie Martin for all her help in the preparation of this final copy.

Andy Hickson

A theatre director, actor and playwright, Andy Hickson has worked in Europe, Africa and Asia, inclding an 18-month stay in the Malaysian rainforest. He also specializes in using action methods to solve difficulties in a variety of settings, such as workplaces, academic institutions, hospitals, schools, youth clubs and community settings. He is a founder member of Tie Tours and a member of the International Society for Intercultural Educaiton (SIETAR). He has published for Routledge, Harwood Academic Publishers and Speechmark Publishing Ltd (formerly Winslow Press).

Part 1

Introduction to groupwork

Chapter 1

Introduction

A group is a system in which 'subjects constantly interact with the results of their own observations and define the systems within which they are embedded' (Long, 1993). This manual is intended for anyone who runs or participates in group sessions. It is a general book on groupwork spanning areas from community groups and social groups to encounter groups and therapeutic groups. How am I going to get the best out of my group? How can I sort out things that go wrong in groups? Which type of group is best for me? What is groupwork? What is a group? These and many other questions will be explored in this manual. The reader will be taken through a broad range of exercises, ideals, pitfalls and descriptions of different methods and systems. The avoidance of jargon means that people will be able to see positive and negative issues surrounding groupwork and how to put theory into practice.

This manual can be used on its own or in conjunction with Winslow's other groupwork manuals, such as *Creative Action Methods in Groupwork*, *Creative Games in Groupwork* and *Creative Drama in Groupwork*.

People and animals often work in groups or packs. Hyenas hunt and scavenge together, which makes them more effective in getting food. A single hyena trying to take prey away from a lion would have little success, whereas ten hyenas working together would probably manage to chase away the lion. Fish swim in shoals, wildebeest travel in giant herds (the more of you there are, the less chance you have of being caught by a shark or a tiger). Likewise, a union of people have more strength than one or two individuals.

> There was a time when all the body's members
> Rebell'd against the belly; thus accus'd it:
> That only like a gulf it did remain
> I' the midst o' the body, idle and inactive,
> Still cupboarding the viand, never bearing
> Like labour with the rest; where the other instruments
> Did see and hear, devise, instruct, walk, feel,
> And, mutually participate, did minister
> Unto the appetite and affection common
> Of the whole body
> (Shakespeare, *Coriolanus*, Act I, Scene 1)

As we develop as humans we learn about ourselves as individuals and as members of a group and of different kinds of groups.

In *developing groups*, groupwork helps us

(a) to develop as individuals and social human beings;
(b) to develop as cultural beings;
(c) to develop as spiritual beings;
(d) to develop our professional identity;
(e) to develop solutions to problems.

There are also groups that help us to make a transition from one state to another, such as college to job or hospital to home. These *transitional groups* can also be rites of passage, most obviously those that symbolize, name, celebrate coming of age, marriage and death. Transitional groups can help us

(a) to move from hospital to home;
(b) to move from nursery to kindergarten;
(c) to move from being single to being paired;
(d) to move from being paired to being a family.

Of course, many of us experience transitions in the other direction, for example from being paired to becoming single, whether through divorce or death. In the past many societies had transitional group rituals as part of the fabric of the society. Few of these now remain, which is why we need to create groups to address this need.

The many types of *interventionist groups* include a number of therapy groups and problem-focused groups; many people would seek out a transitional group, or such a group would be suggested to them, but with interventionist groups there is a conscious act of intervening. For example, I have been asked by a local authority to intervene where there was rivalry between gangs and to design appropriate groupwork for them. Interventionist groups may address the following:

(a) unacceptable behaviour by an individual or community;
(b) failure to thrive at home, work or school;
(c) repetitive mishaps or disasters;
(d) self-destructive behaviour such as cutting or attempted suicide.

Group behaviour and our behaviour within a group have been researched exhaustively over the years. Most of this research is wrapped up in academic jargon and is incomprehensible. Take the question, 'What is a group?' Parsons *et al* (1951) answered in the following way:

> The concept of a boundary is of crucial importance in the definition of a collectivity. The boundary of a collectivity is that criterion whereby some persons are included as members and others are excluded as non-members. The inclusion or exclusion of a person depends on whether or not he has a membership role in the collectivity. Thus all persons who have such roles are members; they are within the boundary. Thus the boundary is defined in terms of membership roles. (1951, p192)

Bales, a year earlier, had stated that a group is: 'Any number of persons engaged in a single face-to-face meeting or a series of meetings in which each member receives some impression of the others as a distinct person even though it was only to recall that the other was present' (Bales, 1950, p33).

Other interpretations are as follows: '*We define a group as a semigroup with an identity in which every element has an inverse*' (Baumslag & Chandler, 1968, p50, emphasis in original) and 'A group is ... the largest set of two or more individuals who are jointly characterised by a network of *relevant* communications, a shared sense of collective identity and one or more shared goal dispositions with normative strengths' (Douglas, 1991, p31, original emphasis).

A zoologist called Jones has a functionalist view; in 1967 he suggested that the group is the *real* existence of which individuals are no more than parts, similar to the cells that go to make up the body, an image evoked by the Shakespeare quotation earlier. Boal says that in a session of the 'theatre of the oppressed':

> Where the participants belong to the same social group ... and suffer the same oppressions, the individual account of a single person will be pluralised: so that the oppression of one is the oppression of all. The particularity of each individual case is negligible in relation to its similarity with all the others. So during the session, sympathy is immediate. *We are all talking about ourselves*. (Boal, 1995, p45, emphasis in original)

Defining what a group is gets even more complicated when people look at large groups, animal groups, gender groups, class groups, age groups, preference groups, social groups, pressure groups, therapy groups, self-help groups and so on.

When looking at the *process* of a group, how a group works, it can be useful to use knowledge about types of group to help us understand how people interact generally. We can find similarities in them all. This has been well documented in other books (see, for example, Douglas, 1976) and so I do not propose to discuss it here. What I do want is to offer a definition of what a group is for the purposes of groupwork:

Two or more people with a leader coming together in a space with the intention of working together (whether by obligation, as in some institutional therapy groups, or by choice, as in some self-help groups or counselling groups).

Chapter 2

Why do we work in groups?

We are social animals; we like to interact with other people. Solitary confinement is looked upon as punishment; as humans we need the contact with others, particularly those of like mind or similar aims and attitudes in life. This is not to say that we should spend all our time in groups. We also need our own space, but people who work or socialize in groups can get an impression of themselves that no amount of looking in the mirror will give them. Without the support and co-operation of others, solitary efforts do not count for much. Some people have found it important to keep the group alive when they are alone. For example, hostages such as Brian Keenan kept the group (family, friends and so on) alive in their heads to keep them going during confinement.

'The group … is not only *interactive* it is also *dynamic*. It is a group whose members are continuously *changing* and *adjusting* relationships with reference to one another (Bonner, 1959, p4, emphasis in original). Trying to bump-start a car is easier with more people pushing. Or is it? If they were all pushing in different directions, they would cancel each other's efforts out and it would all be a waste of energy. If they worked together and all pushed the same way, they would be working as a group and the car would have a good chance of starting.

We are all part of a group. We were born into a group and share many of the values of that group. We also die in groups. People have consciously worked in groups for many reasons over the centuries: groups at war, groups observing rituals, families and so on. All groups have their leaders and much has been written about the relationship between these leaders and their people.

The first recorded use of group therapy as we know it this century was by Joseph Pratt in 1905. He helped tuberculosis patients get together to talk about their struggles with the illness. It was noted that participation in the group mobilized support, gave hope and corrected misinformation. Group therapy was further recorded as being practised in the 1920s by Trigant Burrow, an American psychoanalyst. This was the time when there was a move from exploring the individual towards the studying of relationships between people and how they affect the personality. He wrote a paper, 'The Basis of Group Analysis', in 1928 suggesting that, by using psychoanalytical principles in a group setting, we could uncover the meaning of relationships and interaction. Burrow is widely regarded as the originator of group analysis and a great pioneer in the whole study of small groups. Some of the most significant names in this early developmental period were WR Bion, with his 'basic assumptions'; SH Foulkes, the developer of group analysis and leadership in groups;

Kurt Goldstein, a neurologist who believed that individual neurones in the brain functioned as part of a communicating network; Fritz Perls, the founder of Gestalt therapy; Kurt Lewin, the originator of 'T' groups; Melanie Klein with her concepts of 'collective projection'; and Jacob L Moreno, the founder of Psychodrama. Despite all the pioneering work of these and many others, therapists still generally concentrated on *individual* therapy. Only recently has groupwork been gaining in importance and practice. Those readers who wish to read in depth on specialized groups should refer to the bibliography at the end of the manual.

So groupwork is a modern phenomenon. Therapy groups have grown many different shoots this century. Only recently have therapy groups been challenged and complemented and, strangely enough, by another type of groupwork: the *self-help group*. These groups are often leaderless and avoid authoritarian structures. People with the same problems or difficulties get together to share experiences and survival strategies and to analyse situations. In self-help groups, therefore, there are no gurus, no ultimate leaders.

Some of the pioneers of groupwork have already been mentioned. For introductions to Augusto Boal and the Theatre of the Oppressed, Sue Jennings and Dramatherapy, and Jacob Moreno and Psychodrama, see Hickson (1995). Here, further details about Bion are of interest. Wilfred Bion was influenced by many people, including Klein, Foulkes, Ezriel and Sutherland. An example of the way he worked with groups can be seen in his Northfield experiments. Here, in charge of military personnel who were in need of rehabilitation, Bion got his groups to resolve interpersonal difficulties and take responsibility for their situations. He was successful in rehabilitating them. In these groups he challenged views of what should happen in the army, allowing soldiers to express their resentment of military organization. The authorities could not take this for long and after a few weeks they transferred him.

After the war Bion went to the Tavistock clinic and, using the approach of 'group analysis' developed by Foulkes, he explored further the 'transference' of feelings, attitudes and fantasies with other group members. Bion himself did not lead many therapeutic groups at the Tavistock, although his approach has been very influential. He believed that the only task of the analyst is to interpret group phenomena, not to give guidance. He would offer different ways of looking at and thinking about behaviour. The group, and not specific individuals, would be given support.

Bion believed that groups held three 'basic assumptions'—fight, flight and pairing—and that these basic assumptions bonded group members together, creating security and unity. The group then worked from the co-operation of the members found in the collective group mentality. Contributions from group members are often given unconsciously and Bion thought it important to follow the group intentions rather than the conscious intentions of its individuals.

Groupwork is at present in a boom period. One can now find a group to explore or help with almost any human need or desire; the choice is so large that it is almost impossible to choose just one. (It is worth noting the value of *symbols* in group identity; these come in many forms, such as badges, regalia and costumes.)

At this point you are invited to take pen and paper and to write down all the groups to which you belong. Give a little thought and time to this before reading on.

How many groups did you write down? Think about the various groups where you meet other people: why do you meet; what kind of membership qualifications are there to join the group; how does the group make decisions; what do you get from being a member; what do you give to the group?

This manual will take readers on a journey through a wide range of groupwork practice. Whether the aim is fun, exploration, therapy, teaching, sharing or learning, guidelines will be given to help you get the best out of your group. The following passage is an example of child rearing in a non-western culture. The author is writing from a western viewpoint (why some people go to other cultures to research groups is too big a subject to discuss here); nevertheless it contains some useful pointers:

> The Senoi ... child is taught in infancy to gain recognition by developing his individual powers of expression along every line which will, in any way, be useful to the group. He is taught both by word of mouth and by example to cooperate and to oppose his fellows when he feels he must oppose them in a spirit of good will. He is taught never to cause pain to any living thing which is in his power, never to cause hunger or desire without helping to assuage and satisfy it, never to cause worry in his fellows by unpredictable and irregular behaviour ... I regard the Senoi pattern as a cultural exploitation of the disassociated state [dreams] which permits an expression and a socialization of the psychological elements of the human personality to an extent which has seldom, if ever, been attained in human

history ... We find a society untainted by violent habits and inter-group conflicts. Moreover, crimes of passion, slavery, black magic, secret societies and tyrants have no place in their daily life ... Psychological health and social well being are dependent on the coordination of the personality with the social group rather than upon the rational or mystic quality of thinking which the individual has. (Stewart, 1947, p34)

Chapter 3

Principles and procedures

Groups are formed for a multitude of reasons. Many of us make a choice to join a group when we have a difficulty of some kind or if we want to improve our skills. We want to mix with people of like mind, sharing stories and experiences in an effort to make sense of our lives. We may want to learn a new skill or polish up an old one. The choice is endless.

Each individual is different, not only in physical appearance, but in dress, origin, thoughts, abilities, sexuality and so on. If follows that each group is going to be different also. Groups can have obvious differences in connection with their subject matter – a dance group will differ greatly from an assertiveness skills training group – but we can go further than this: two dance groups could differ greatly in their styles, as with a Kathakali dance group and a ballroom dancing group. We can go further still: two ballroom dance groups could differ in style of leadership, size of class, regularity of meeting, commitment of members, length of time together, background of members, funds available and so on.

Despite all these differences, it is important to recognize that there are many similarities as well. The above examples could have just as many similarities cited as differences. It is all a matter of perception, our perception. Some people think that working in a group is a way of 'doing it on the cheap', that working individually must be better. This is often not the case; people need to understand that working in groups can actually be better. We cannot be totally the same as someone else, nor can we be totally different from someone else; each of us is slightly different in our own way. Just as with individual differences and similarities, so too with groups. Two similar groups will have differences. Two similar people in the same group will have differences. Two different groups will have similarities. Two different people in the same group will have similarities. If we have a difficulty and we cannot sort it out ourselves, it is often appropriate to turn to others for help and support. Finding a group where the members suffer similar difficulties could be our answer. Finding a group where the members have enough similarities to us could be the answer. Whatever our criterion, we join a group so that we can get something back from it.

We have a vast number of groups from which to choose. Choosing a group is a two-way process: we can choose the group we wish to join but we must also fit the group's selection criteria. For example, if the group has a rule of not admitting anyone over 30 years of age and we are 40, then, unless we lie, we do not stand a chance of getting in. If we do not like the choices available to us, we can start a new group to meet our demands. This may sound easy but, almost invariably, it is not. If we want to set up our own group we need people to join to make it a group; we need to attract enough people with enough similarities to us that they want to join this group and not some other group. Groups have often started out of personal crisis or tragedy, perhaps from a need to find out information that is not forthcoming, or as a way of finding support in coping with incurable disease, the loss of a relative or a false imprisonment. These groups can continue long after the original person's trauma has been relieved, because other people have joined and have carried the group forward.

All groups have processes that they go through and it is widely held that all groups have essentially the same dynamic bases and grow at different levels of intensity in the direction they are pushed. There is much debate about what these processes are. What actually happens within a group? How are decisions made, for example? Again each group is different and reaches decisions in the ways that work well for it. The direction a group is going to take depends, amongst other things, on the style of leadership employed.

Leadership

How many leaders can you think of? What kind of people are they? Do they all have similar qualities? How do they get their support? How a group is led is one of the most important factors in determining the nature of a group. Ways to lead a group are many and various: differences in emphasis, with one group leader promoting individual effort within the group and another choosing to promote an awareness of responsibility for the group; differences of projection, with some group leaders keeping quiet while others are loud; differences even of title: group leader, facilitator, conductor, guide, tutor, joker, and so on.

As each group is different, with different needs and different purposes, careful consideration needs to be given to the leadership style that most suits the individual and the group. We are going to look at three kinds of leaders: those in *task-centred groups*, those in *art/action-centred groups* and those in *talk-centred groups*.

The leader in task-centred groups is usually going to place emphasis on the process an individual has to go through rather than on the process the group has to go through. The leader will be imparting social skills such as assertiveness training or problem-solving training to individuals who are working within a group setting and must be flexible so as to tailor techniques to the needs of each particular client. Many task-centred groups have a leader and a co-leader, often of the opposite sex. This is recommended, as the presence of leaders of both sexes helps the

modelling of behaviours from different perspectives. The group leaders are educators; they are there not only to make sure the group reaches its goals but also to teach their clients skills, such as coping with stress, learning to be assertive or changing specific behaviour patterns.

The leader at art/action-centred groups is often going to place emphasis on the process of the group rather than on an individual's process. This energetic leader will need to be confident and outgoing, with a huge measure of sensitivity. The leader will actively steer the group with, for example, the use of group games, exercises, set texts and improvisation to explore and solve issues and difficulties in people's lives. This leader is not an educator as such but more of a director, setting limits, encouraging open interaction, protecting individuals from intimidation but letting the group reach its own decisions, explore its own issues and find its own solutions. Boal (1992) says: 'the Joker [group leader] is a midwife ... of body and spirit ... [and] must assist the birth of all ideas, of all actions'.

The leader in talk-centred groups must love analysing the 'truth' with the help of the group. The aim of the group is to free its individuals of conflicts and help with the difficulties they may have in their relationships with other people. The leader (or the conductor, as they are often called) will help provide a safe space where the group may play with ideas, metaphors and symbols. The leader should have a strong feeling for language, including the exploration of verbal slips, swearing, sighs and the choice of vocabulary each member uses. Leaders do not have all the answers and often show themselves as being on the same journey of discovery as other group members.

Not all groups will fit neatly into these three categories. In fact most groups, like most people, will be unable to fit into any category and the effective leader will often have skills pertaining to a wide variety of groupwork. There is no such thing as the perfect group leader, but there are many characteristics that can help a leader accomplish a great deal. The leader who is enthusiastic, energized, open to feelings, interested in people and open to their potential to change and grow, and who can avoid falling into the trap of providing all the answers, will be extremely effective. The group leader should

(a) have adequate training for the task and in the skills to be imparted;
(b) believe that group members will help each other;
(c) have an ability to talk clearly and openly to groups;
(d) have a good memory for the names of the group members;

(e) have an ability to recognize and to link themes, difficulties and issues;

(f) ensure that participants are rewarded with praise for their efforts, if appropriate;

(g) have an ability to shape inappropriate responses without rejecting them as wrong;

(h) have an ability to monitor non-verbal behaviour and act accordingly;

(i) have an ability to steer participants towards the job in hand;

(j) know when to be directive and when not;

(k) know his or her personal limits and blindspots;

(l) enjoy the group.

The group leader should *not* abuse his or her power, manipulate the group for personal gain, pride or ego trip, or place group members in child-like dependency.

Choosing a group

Groupwork can take us as far as we want to go. We may choose to take little steps at first and, if this is successful, larger steps may be taken. Have we joined a group to receive therapy? Have we joined a group to learn new skills? Have we joined a group to explore difficulties in our lives? Do we just want to have fun? Do we want to change in some way?

Many groups outside institutionalized care do not see their members as patients to be cured. Therapy groups such as Dramatherapy, Psychodrama and Gestalt see their members as people or as clients; leaders of cognitive-behavioural groups see their members as customers; self-help group leaders often see their group members as fellow-sufferers. Many groups offer experiences which are not meant to be therapy but which turn out to be therapeutic.

There is no strict formula for choosing the 'right' group, but if we take the following steps we will not go far wrong:

1 Decide why we want to join a group, perhaps listing our aims.

2 Look for groups that have similar aims and objectives to our own.

3 Talk to members or leaders from groups that appeal to us.

4 Do not be afraid to ask questions.

5 Ask to look at results, reports, evaluations or any literature that the group or group leader might have.

6 If we do not find what we want, we have the possibility of starting up our own group.

7 If the group does not 'work' for us, feel free to change it.

If we decide to set up our own group, we should ask ourselves the following questions:

Are there enough resources to start the group?
Do I have support from other organizations?
Where will the group be held?
Who will be responsible for what?
What happens in case of accidents or emergencies?
Will I be able to get suitable members?
What are the aims of the group?
What type of group will it be?
Will the group be open or closed?
What will be the group focus?
What will the size of the group be?
How many leaders will the group use?
How often will the group meet?
How long will the sessions be?
How will members be selected?
How will the group be publicized?

Sensitive groups

Some people are very sensitive and often wear this sensitivity on their sleeve. Others have ways of disguising their sensitivity, such as layers of body mass or clothes, avoidance or aggression. An enabling group leader should, on the one hand, be aware of sensitive issues in an individual's life, but on the other be able to run a robust group in which everyone can find strength.

People come to groups for a variety of reasons, and many who do indeed need personal counselling see coming to a group as a less threatening way of seeking help. Other people come to groups with one idea which may be masking others. For example, someone may join a group in order to improve their confidence, when the underlying reason may be that they have no confidence because they 'were never wanted anyway'. To illustrate the point, Geoff came to the group to be more confident but spent most of the time being as obnoxious as possible, attacking people verbally and generally being very unpleasant. The group got extremely angry with him and at one point a woman suddenly shouted at him: "Anyone would think that you didn't want us to like you." The man crumpled and burst into tears. The group leader understood that Geoff was enacting his past situations of not being wanted. He was not in need of long-term therapy; in fact this was the breakthrough he needed and he was able to address the issues in the group.

Groups which are run in hospitals for people with mental health problems will need careful planning and clinical advice from medical staff, as well as some knowledge of the background of the group members. However, the greatest guide to potential sensitivity is the group itself and all its members. The leader of sensitive groups will learn through experience to tune in to the themes and dynamics of the group. A good motto to remember is: 'If in doubt, ask the group.'

Different groups

As we have already said, each group is different. Every group has different aims, boundaries, directions, membership and so on. Although each group is different, many of the techniques and approaches involved are similar. Self-help groups, Gestalt group therapy, group analysis, interpersonal group therapy, Psychodrama, Dramatherapy and cognitive-behavioural group therapy are some of the small groups that people work in and from which most of the information about good groupwork comes.

Self-help groups are usually loose, voluntary associations of people, whose general activities are directed towards common goals such as coping with illness, social or psychological difficulties by which they or relatives are affected. These groups are usually non-profit making. They meet regularly (once a week or once a month) sharing and giving mutual aid. Self-help groups are not usually run by professional workers but they do consult experts on certain questions that may crop up.

Members join a Gestalt group because they want to live less painful or more fulfilling lives. Maladaptive behaviours of individuals are often broken down by the group as members work towards greater contact with themselves and each other.

In group analysis the member is encouraged to have a greater awareness of their thoughts and feelings and to develop their full potential to help their future relationships.

Interpersonal group therapy allows individuals to bring their own recurrent interpersonal difficulties to the group. The group forms a laboratory where all these interactions are analysed and where new resolutions may be practised. A sense of meaning and purpose in life is strengthened through the exercise of responsibility and choice.

In Psychodrama the group allows a space where spontaneous creative experimentation can take place. Members act out roles of people important in their lives and sides of themselves that they do not usually show. Fuller and warmer understanding of roles and counter-roles are reached and avoided feelings are expressed.

Dramatherapy is similar in many ways to Psychodrama, but it does have some very important differences, one being the emphasis of the group: in Psychodrama, one is working with the problem or difficulty of an individual; in Dramatherapy, a dramatic distance is created; instead of working on an individual's problem, a story is found that will capture everyone's difficulty. For example the story of *King Lear* could be used to look at the difficulty of family relationships. This safe distance often brings the group closer.

Cognitive-behavioural group therapy tries to modify particular difficult cognitions and behaviours put forward by clients, who are then taught how they should manage feelings of anxiety and how to improve their social skills.

Chapter 4

Overcoming difficulties

What is a difficulty? The word obviously has many interpretations. Difficulties are different for each person and for each group and are all relative to the situation in hand. We often come to groups because we have a difficulty of some kind that we want to explore or to overcome. Once in the group it does not mean that all our problems will go away; in fact the group setting may generate more difficulties as we prepare to face the problem. This is a fact of life as it is a fact of groups, but how can we overcome difficulties in the process that the group is taking? How can we recognize that there are difficulties presenting themselves within the group? Is the leader to blame? Are individuals to blame? Is the group to blame? Is anyone to blame?

Difficulties in the group process can arise with any group. Even the best working group has difficulties and it is in overcoming these difficulties that groups very often make progress. When problems arise, it is very important not to hide from them; if we brush them aside they will return and manifest themselves in even more negative ways. If a problem is there we must face it, ask the group what they think about it, look at it from different angles, discuss how it happened and what we are going to do about it, and so on.

Let us look at some of the problems that can arise. First, relevant training is essential: running a group can be scary, especially in the early stages, and, if the trainer has not acquired the necessary skills, people can be harmed, particularly in sensitive groups. A second problem is lack of planning. Groups that have not been planned well from the start are liable to get into many difficulties. Such groups include the one that meanders through whim after whim without ever facing anything, the group that gets nothing done because it has no time, and the group that has no space to meet in because it has not been booked. Third, a group with no boundaries can have people turning up late or not at all, not caring about the group and 'doing their own thing'. Finally, problems may arise over the choice of members. In many circumstances the size of the group and who can join should be given careful attention. Is the group a *closed* one, where members stay together for the entire life of the group: an intense, shared, complete experience of starting, working together and ending? Or is it an *open* group, which people can join when a vacancy arises? Is there a good balance in the group? If members are given false impressions or false expectations, this can lead to recriminations later on.

There are a number of common difficulties that a group leader may have to face in the course of a session. Often the group will consist of sullen and unresponsive members who just want to sit there, or who want to be negative, or who do not want to be there at all. What, if anything, can be done to get the group moving? If someone does not want to be involved then we cannot force them. Whatever we do might not be enough for some people. On the other hand, we could be the reason for the group being as it is. There are many ways to go forwards, but which path to take will depend on the group in question. A group working together over a long period will have more time to explore difficulties. The leader should try and feel or understand what the group is saying, even if it is saying it through silence. Is the silence vengeful or defensive? Is the hostility of the group a recurring problem? What happened in the last group session? Has the group got the right mix of people? How did the group solve problems before? Is the group warmed up? Has the group had a chance to brush away cobwebs and break down barriers? Do people feel safe? Has something happened outside the group? Is the leader being used as a scapegoat? Have things been promised that cannot be realized? Are individual needs taking precedence over the group needs?

Someone in a group may ask the leader a question which it is appropriate to answer, but the leader does not know the answer. In such a situation, the leader should not be afraid of saying that they do not know. Maybe someone else in the group knows the answer?

Sometimes people will have hidden motives for making a contribution to the group. They may say something for the sake of saying it, or they may be trying to manipulate the group, or individuals in the group, into going in certain directions or into believing certain things that are not true. People do this for many reasons, often ones that they do not know themselves. It is important for the leader and/or the group to recognize when this is happening and to take appropriate action, usually by confronting the group with the dilemma.

People who are absent and therefore unable to defend themselves are sometimes criticized in the group session. This is to be avoided at all costs: usually the person will hear what has gone on, some time later, and this may well cause more problems than there were at first.

There are very few clinicians who work with large group psychotherapy. (Dr Patrick de Maré is one of the few specialists in this field.) Large groups can have large problems. Groups such as school assemblies, seminars and shareholders' meetings exist for specific purposes. Usually they simply confirm that a particular body of people exist or are used to inform, rather than harnessing skills or generating work. Hostility in a large group can take a variety of forms and can quite easily mutate and grow if left unchecked. Dramatization of these hostilities to the group can often be effective in successful explorations, forms of individual activity negotiated in public. For example, group difficulties often result in someone being held up as a scapegoat. Dramatizing this to the group can often bring new perspectives, so that we can see how much the scapegoat's 'sins' really belong to the whole group. *Action methods* are an excellent way of working in this sense (see Hickson, 1995).

A group may be lacking in energy, focus and commitment. If the reason is not apparent, a change of activity can often energize the group. One area to look at is the idea of a pre-group warm-up. Any group, whether task-based, action-based or talk-based, can warm up. A brief warm-up at the beginning of a session loosens up the voice, the body and the mind.

Sometimes a small minority may disrupt the group activity. This is a problem of many groups, particularly those where people have not actively made the choice to be there. This could include institutionalist groups, school groups, probation groups and so on. Try and find out what the difficulty is and see if an activity can be found in which the whole group can participate. If this is not possible and the members who do not want to join in cannot leave, use the problem directly as a focus for the work. For example, when they do not want to join in, some people complain that they are bored. If this is the case, try finding out what they would rather be doing. Often the reply is "nothing". If people want to do nothing, it is possible to explore what nothing is and to ask how people can do nothing. If we just sit in a chair, we are not doing nothing because we are sitting in a chair, which is doing something! Who can do nothing the best?

Some leaders have difficulty in getting the right relationship with their group from the start. These leaders may often blame the group rather than themselves if things go badly. Johnstone (1979, p29) says that it is essential for teachers to blame themselves if the group are not in a good state:

The first thing I do when I meet a group of students is to sit on the floor. I play low status, and I'll explain that if the students fail they're to blame *me*. Then they laugh, and relax, and I explain that really it's obvious that they should blame me, since I'm supposed to be the expert; and if I give them the wrong material, they'll fail; and if I give them the right material, then they'll succeed. I play low status physically but my actual status is going up, since only a very confident and experienced person would put the blame for failure on themselves. At this point they almost certainly start sliding off their chairs, because they don't want to be higher than me. I have already changed the group profoundly, because failure is suddenly not so frightening any more. They'll want to test me, of course; but I really will apologise to them if they fail, and ask them to be patient with me, and explain that I'm not perfect … most students will succeed, but they won't be trying to win any more. The normal teacher–student relationship is dissolved.

Groupwork with young children is often very different from working with adolescents and adults. Young children usually express their feelings through play activity, whereas older people tend to use language as the main channel for communicating feelings. Play activity is also an excellent method of keeping control of a young children's group. The rules that are inherent in all games can add structure and direction to any group. If the group has trouble in giving in to control, games with little prior direction are a good place to start. Examples are hide-and-seek, storytelling, tag and so on. As the group becomes more able to handle rules, games with higher levels of prior direction can be introduced. Do not think that rules in a game are fixed: they are not; rules can be changed to suit the need of the group. Games can be made more or less complex; they can be converted from being competitive to being co-operative, or vice versa. For example, a game of tag, where someone is 'it' and tries by chasing after the others and touching one of them to make them 'it' as well, can be quite competitive. If we change the rules just slightly and allow people to be delivered from being 'it', by someone else in the group crawling through their legs for example, we have added an element of co-operation. This can then be built upon if desired. 'Games provide an opportunity for the child to learn the consequences of his actions without having to suffer them. In a game mistakes and exposure of ignorance are more tolerated. Games usually encourage laughing and joking, which can be instrumental in relieving anxiety and facilitating involvement' (Cartledge & Milburn, 1981, p100).

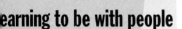
earning to be with people

Every group has a mirror image and one of the functions of a healthy group is to find a balance between the needs of the individual and the needs of the group as a whole. Appropriate techniques and group structure will help members to find this balance. When a problem does arise, it can be useful to try and find the mirror image and explore it within the group. Starting off with the question, 'Why do people come to groups?' leads to the following ten examples of mirror images.

Question	Mirror
1 Do I irritate people?	Am I intolerant of people?
2 Do I touch people inappropriately?	Have I told people I do not like being touched?
3 Do I have difficulty communicating with others?	Do I listen to what others are saying?
4 Am I shy?	Do I exploit my shyness in order to gain attention?
5 Do I want to meet people?	Am I rigid about the people I want to meet?
6 Do I scare people off?	Am I easily frightened?
7 Do I want to be like other people?	Do I enjoy my individuality?
8 Do I do things I do not want to do?	Do I find it easier for other people to make decisions?
9 Am I really unattractive?	Am I scared of being attractive?
10 Do I want to learn something?	Do I want to teach something?

Chapter 5

The voice

Our voice is unique and unerringly reflects how we feel both physically and emotionally. As with any muscular action, to get the best out of our voice we need to keep it flexible and exercised. The exercises later in this chapter will help you achieve this.

Actors, more than anyone, know that to get the best out of our voice we need to train it regularly and they often spend hours a day on voice exercises, just as an athlete will spend hours a day training to run a 100 metres race. Much of the pioneering work on voice production has come from the theatre, from people such as Stanislavski, Volkonski and Ushakov. In the early 1900s, Stanislavski told his actors to think about the strength of speech rather than the volume. This strength was to be found in the intonations and range of a voice, not in its loudness or in shouting. Stanislavski wanted his actors to use the whole spectrum of sound available to them. To do this he devised a phonetic alphabet where the sensation of each sound and syllable could be explored.

Jerzy Grotowski's approach to voice training was a rejection of the perfect diction that was taught at most drama schools; rather he wanted the voice to enter the audience as if it were stereophonic, so that even the walls would resound with the actor's voice. Many of Grotowski's exercises derived from classical Chinese theatre or Hatha yoga and a lot of time was spent developing the resonators important in voice production.

F Mathias Alexander believed that exercising the voice was not just a matter of training the vocal organs; it meant training the whole body, posture, breathing and one's state of mind. Born in 1869 in Australia, he was an actor whose voice failed him in performances. In an attempt to find out why, he spent a long time on self-observation, including breathing methods and body posture. His findings were of great value and use outside the theatre. In certain instances his techniques offered patients an alternative to surgery. In 1904, Alexander set up a practice in London. In 1930, a training course for teachers of his method, the 'Alexander Technique', was established and his findings were published two years later. Alexander influenced many people and the Alexander Technique is taught in many places today. An important concept to be remembered from Alexander's work is that the body can be re-educated and freed from unhelpful or habitual patterns of response.

To use our voices well does not mean that we have to spend hours a day exercising them but we can spend minutes a day doing so. This will help us to achieve three things: (1) producing our voice without hurting ourselves; (2) a voice that is flexible and able to convey what we want to convey; and (3) an ability to use our voices fully for several

hours a day and having it as free and flexible at the end of the day as it was at the beginning.

Some speech problems can be improved with practice, although many problems, such as a lisp, stuttering or the effects of a cleft palate, should be treated by a speech and language therapist. However, undue tension in the vocal tract and the articulators will inhibit voice and speech, so reducing tension in the neck, jaw and face will produce a fuller, more resonant sound. For some stutterers, reducing tension areas may help them to achieve easier speech production, but this is not always the case.

A general exercise routine to improve most aspects of speech and voice production

1 Before starting it is very important to loosen up physically.

  (a) Stretch: spend five minutes stretching your feet, ankles, legs, torso, arms and neck; do not overdo it; limber up gently.
  (b) Yawn: loosen the area around the head, neck and shoulders.
  (c) Blow raspberries.

2 Breath is the power behind the voice. When speaking, we need to ensure an adequate supply of oxygen to the blood and sufficient breath of the right pressure to pass through the glottis and the speech organs and give us the appropriate volume control.

  (a) Breathe out through the mouth to a slow count of six, then relax to breathe in through the nose.
  (b) On one breath, whisper a count to ten; breathe in again and then whisper on one breath to 15; breathe in again and then whisper on one breath to 20, letting the breath flow on easily.
  (c) Repeat (b), counting at normal volume.
  (d) Repeat (b), counting loudly.

3 The resonators enrich our voices, adding warmth, colour, body and audibility. We also use some resonators such as the nose to differentiate sounds such as nasalized vowels (although not usually in English) and the consonants n, m and ŋ.

  (a) With the teeth apart and lips just touching, hum gently, feeling the vibration of the hum forwards over the front of the face.
  (b) Repeat (a), using higher and lower notes.
  (c) Repeat (a), increasing and decreasing the volume.
  (d) Hum before saying each of the following words, letting the word be placed 'forwards' in the same way that the hum is placed 'forwards':

  many mighty men making money in the moonshine.

  Repeat five times.
  (e) Count from one to ten, feeling the back of the mouth lifting (as when yawning).

(f) Count again to ten, this time feeling the sound vibrating in the body and the chest.

(g) Hold your nose and count from one to ten without making it sound as if you are holding your nose.

(h) Say the following, letting the sound resonate through your cavities:

ah, ay, ee, ay, ah, or, oo, or, ah.

Now go through the alphabet, putting the same letter first at the beginning, then the end and then both together; for example, 'Z' will give the following:

Zah, Zay, Zee, Zay, Zah, Zor, Zoo, Zor, Zah.
ahZ, ayZ, eeZ, ayZ, ahZ, orZ, ooZ, orZ, ahZ.
ZahZ, ZayZ, ZeeZ, ZayZ, ZahZ, ZorZ, ZooZ, ZorZ, ZahZ.

4 The way we pronounce our words is important for making ourselves understood. The following exercises help ensure clear speech.

(a) Gently draw your hands down your face, letting your jaw drop open.

(b) Open and close your mouth many times, letting your jaw drop open easily, repeating 'pah, pah, pah', audibly or silently.

(c) Loosen the lips and tongue by sticking your tongue out several times and rolling it around your mouth. Blow a few more raspberries.

(d) Silently or aloud, repeat the following, rapidly and precisely:

WBW (ten times)
WVW (five times)
WVBW (five times)

(e) Relax the jaw, keeping your teeth apart. Take the tip of the tongue from behind the upper teeth to behind the lower teeth and repeat:

LLL LLL LLL (five times)
DDD DDD DDD (five times)
LDL LDL LDL (five times)

5 Giving our voices variety not only helps us to be understood but also adds colour to our voices, which encourages people to listen to them.

(a) Count from one to nine, giving each number a rising inflection.
(b) Count from one to nine, giving each number a falling inflection.
(c) Count from one to nine alternating up and down inflections.

An enjoyable way of exercising our voices is to play around with tongue twisters. For a comprehensive selection, see Hickson (1995). The following exercises are an excellent way of warming and toning up the voice.

Transforming sound

Aim: Exploring and expressing emotion, voice exercise

Time: 10–15 minutes

Materials and preparation: The group should be warmed up and at ease with each other.

Activity: Ask the group to get into pairs. Ask each pair to share an action, such as starting a car, blowing your nose and so on. One of the partners now adds a sound to go with the action. After several moments the other partner moves away and transforms the action and sound into something of their own. This person is encouraged to experience this sound and action emotionally and to express it physically.

People are enabled by this activity to make themselves vulnerable to difficult emotions and are allowed to express these emotions in sound and movement rather than saying what they feel.

After a hug, ask the partners to swap roles.

Closure: Invite the group into a circle and make a huge hug. Talk with the group about the emotions released. How do the group feel?

NB This game is not recommended for use with sensitive groups.

Blowing each other out

Aim: Breath control, movement

Time: 5 minutes

Materials and preparation: None

Activity: Ask the group to get into pairs. One partner pretends to be a candle flame; the other tries to blow him out. The first partner should move as if he were a flame being blown and if he is blown out he should curl up in a ball. After a few minutes, ask pairs to swap over and repeat the activity.

Closure: Talk with the group about how they feel.

Volume

Volume control, attention keeping

5 minutes

None

Ask the group to split into pairs. Each person should now think up a short sentence about anything and repeat it to their partner so that each partner knows what their partner's sentence is. Everyone meets in the centre, then slowly walks backwards away from their partner, repeating their sentence to their partner. As they walk backwards they must increase the volume of their sentence (without shouting) so that partners can hear each other. When they are as far as possible away from their partner, they stop saying that sentence and try to have a conversation at a distance. After a few minutes, bring the group into a circle.

Talk with the group about how they feel. Could they hear each other above other people? Were they able to have a conversation?

Questions

Aim:

Time:

Materials and preparation:

Activity:

Variation:

Closure:

Using the voice, creativity

5–10 minutes

None

Invite the group to get into pairs. Each participant must try and have a conversation with their partner but all replies should be in the form of a question. After a few minutes, participants change partners and do the same again.

As above, but replies should be as if participants are answering a question.

Talk with the group about how they feel.

Singing questions

Aim: Playing with the voice, creativity

Time: 5–10 minutes

Materials and preparation: None

Activity: Everyone should get into pairs and have a conversation. Participants sing their conversations; all replies should be in the form of a question. After a few minutes, change partners and do the same again.

Closure: Talk with the group about how they feel.

Balloons

Aim: Breath control

Time: 10 minutes

Materials and preparation: None

Activity: Ask the group to get into threes. One person in the group is a balloon and the other two blow the balloon up, using long outbreaths. When the balloon is fully inflated, the other two play blow ping-pong by blowing the balloon back and forth between them. The person playing the balloon moves faster or slower, depending on the strength of the blowing directed at them. After a little while, ask participants to swap roles and do the same again. Continue until everyone has had a go at being the balloon.

Closure: Talk with the group about how they feel.

Part 2

Methods, techniques and presentation

Chapter 6

Methods, techniques and

Finding the right ice-breaker or warm-up for your
difficulties for even the most experienced group lea
people feel at ease and draw them out to want to co
and open themselves up? There is no magic formula
time for all groups.

Some group leaders like to jump straight into 'doin   ne group
should be doing'; others like to have an introductory period, offering an
outline of the session, with the participants introducing themselves to
each other. One of the easiest ways of breaking the ice with a 'one off'
workshop, the first session of a new group or an influx of new members is
to play a game. The following activities provide a variety of warm-up games
and ice-breakers.

Name game

Aim: To break the ice, have fun and to learn group members' names

Time: 10 minutes

Materials and preparation: A small ball, such as a ball used for juggling

Activity: The leader should ask the group to stand in a circle and then ask each person to say their name. The leader now explains that they are going to play a short name memory game and gives the following advice: "Whoever throws the ball must call out the name of the person they are throwing it to, and whoever receives the ball must call out the name of the person who threw it to them. If a name is forgotten at any time, that person should repeat their name and the person who forgot it should also then repeat it. You can throw the ball to whoever you want, as long as it is a different person each time." The leader starts the game by saying the name of a member and then throwing them the ball. The game ends when all names have been remembered or when the group think it is appropriate.

Variation: As above, but with participants sitting in chairs.

Closure: The leader should talk with the group members about how they feel.

Name paint

Aim: Ice breaking, fun and remembering group members' names

Time: 5 minutes

Materials and preparation: None

Activity: The group leader should ask the group members to stand facing each other in two lines. Name one line A and the other B. Get line A to write or paint their name in the air to the person opposite them in line B. Each person in line B should then say the name of the person opposite them; if it is right it is answered with a smile, if it is wrong then person A repeats the name verbally and so does person B. Repeat, with line B starting. Line B then moves one person to the left, with the person at the far left (who now has no-one facing them) going to the other end of the line to face a new partner in line A. Repeat the whole process until everyone has painted their name.

Variations: As above, but sitting down.
Group members paint an imaginary mascot as well as their name.

Closure: The leader talks with the group about how they feel.

Stretch out of the cobwebs

Aim: Body awareness, warm-up

Time: 5 minutes

Materials and preparation: None

Activity: The leader encourages the members to form a circle and then verbally identifies parts of the body in turn and suggests a gradual stretch and relaxation for each named part, working through the body from top to bottom, left to right, bottom to top or without obvious order: toes, foot, ankle, toes, foot, ankle, knee, knee, leg, leg, thighs, waist, chest, back, shoulders, elbows, arms, wrists, fingers, hands, neck, head.

Variation: As above, but sitting down.

Closure: The leader asks the group to slowly touch their toes and slowly come back up to a standing position and then asks them how they feel.

Breathing out

Aim: Release of stress, breaking the ice

Time: 3 minutes

Materials and preparation: None

Activity: The leader asks the group to form a circle, with each person's feet their shoulders' width apart and touching the side of the foot of the person next to them on either side. With knees slightly bent, everyone closes their eyes. The leader says: "Breathe in for a count of three seconds, one … two … three; hold it for a count of two seconds, one … two; breathe out slowly for a count of eight seconds into the centre of the circle, one … two … three … four … five … six … seven … eight; breathe normally again." This should be repeated five times.

Variation: As above, breathing out to a count of ten, 12, 15 and 20.

Closure: The leader asks the group how they feel.

Names and the now

Aim: Ice breaking, grounding the group in the present

Time: 5 minutes

Materials and preparation: None

Activity: The leader asks the group to form a circle. Each member in turn is then prompted to say their name, turn round in the circle and then name something they have noticed. The group as a whole should then repeat that person's name and the thing they noticed.

Variation: As above, but sitting down.

Closure: The leader asks the group how they feel.

My name is Andy and I like animation

Aim: Ice breaking, remembering group members' names

Time: 3 minutes

Materials and preparation: None

Activity: The leader should get the group to form a circle. Each person in turn is then invited to say their name and then something they like beginning with the same letter as their first initial. The group then repeats the name and the thing liked. For example: "My name is John and I like journeys; my name is Selina and I like singing; my name is Pete and I like pointed shoes."

Variation: As above, but sitting down.

Closure: The leader asks the group how they feel.

Name intro

Aim: Ice breaking, remembering group members' names, speaking in front of the group

Time: 5 minutes

Materials and preparation: None

Activity: The leader should invite the group to form a line at one end of the space, all facing the far end. The leader explains that, one after the other, each person will come out of the line and face the rest of the group. They will then, in this order, thank the preceding member (unless they are the first), greet the group verbally in any fashion they desire, say their own name and then say, "I would now like to welcome a fellow member", before returning to the line. The next person comes up, repeats the procedure and so on until the last member has spoken. For example: "Thank you for that introduction, Sergie. Hello, friends, my name is Constance. I would now like to welcome a fellow member."

Variation: As above, but sitting down.

Closure: The leader asks the group how they feel.

Oh! Hello

Aim: Ice breaking, brushing away cobwebs

Time: 3 minutes

Materials and preparation: None

Activity: The leader should invite the group to form a line at one end of the space, all facing the far end. The leader explains that, one after the other, each person will come out of the line and face the rest of the group. They will then, in this order, close their eyes, slump their shoulders, breathe deeply into the stomach and then have a huge yawn, reaching their hands up to the ceiling. After the yawn they should open their eyes and say to the group, with mock surprise: "Oh! Hello." They then return to the line and the next person repeats the process. And so on.

Variations: As above, but sitting down.
Add vocalizations to the yawn.

Closure: The leader should ask everyone to do a group yawn, shake the body out and ask the group how they feel.

Chat line

Aim: Ice breaking, getting to know people's names

Time: 5 minutes

Materials and preparation: None

Activity: The leader asks the group to form a circle and sit down. The leader gives one of the members an imaginary telephone and says to them: "I want you to ring a number and make the sound of the bell until someone in the group answers the phone." The rest of the group is then told that anyone may answer the phone by saying: "Hello, who is that?" When this happens, the person ringing tells them their name and asks the receiver theirs. They both then say goodbye. The receiver then takes the imaginary phone and starts the process again. People may answer the phone up to two times each. The game ends when everyone has had a go at ringing and receiving.

Variation: In pairs, participants have a short conversation with each other on the telephone.

Closure: The leader talks with the group about how they feel.

Nonsense?

Aim: Ice breaking, releasing stress, giving names

Time: 5 minutes

Materials and preparation: A watch with a second hand

Activity: The leader asks the group to form a circle and explains to them that, apart from telling each other their names, they will speak nothing but nonsense words in this exercise. The leader invites one person at a time into the centre of the circle. They are asked to say their names and then to speak continuous nonsense words for 30 seconds. The leader is timekeeper and says: "Start ... 20 to go ... 10 to go ... five to go ... stop." The group then thank this person by name. The group member rejoins the circle and the next person follows the same procedure. This goes on until everyone has had a go.

Variations: The group can reply in nonsense language.
Set up nonsense dialogues.

Closure: The leader asks the group how they feel.

What is their name?

Aim: Ice breaking, name sharing, memorizing

Time: 5 minutes

Materials and preparation: None

Activity: The leader asks the group to form a circle and to sit down. Each person in turn speaks their name several times. Before going on, allow a few seconds for people to look at each other. One at a time, participants stand up, with their backs to the group, and another person describes a group member. The person standing up tries to guess the name of the person being described. When the name has been guessed, the person standing up sits down and another follows the same procedure. Continue until everyone has had a go.

Variation: As above, but participants sing the words instead of speaking them.

Closure: The leader asks the group how they feel.

An immovable object 1

Aim: Ice breaking, awareness of others, name remembering

Time: 10 minutes

Materials and preparation: None

Activity: In this game people are trying not to win or to lose. The leader starts by dividing the group into pairs. Each pair finds a space in the room away from the others. They then face each other, putting their palms in front of them so that they touch their partner's palms. They then introduce themselves to their partner by saying: "My name is … and I'm going to push you over." Each person pushes their partner as hard as they can, but they must not push them over. They must be aware of their partner's strength and push just enough so as not to push them over. After 30 seconds, they all change partners and repeat the process, until they have all met and pushed each other.

Variation: As above, but sitting down.

Closure: The leader talks with the group about how they feel.

An immovable object 2

Aim: Ice breaking, awareness of others, name remembering

Time: 10 minutes

Materials and preparation: None

Activity: In this game people are trying not to win or to lose. The leader starts by dividing the group into pairs. Each pair finds a space in the room away from the others. They stand back to back and then introduce themselves to their partner by saying: "My name is … and I'm going to push you over." Each person pushes their partner as hard as they can, but they must not push them over. They must be aware of their partner's strength and push just enough so as not to push them over. After 30 seconds, they all change partners and repeat the process, until they have all met and pushed each other.

Variation: As above, but sitting on the floor.

Closure: The leader talks with the group about how they feel.

An immovable object 3

Aim: Ice breaking, awareness of others, name remembering

Time: 10 minutes

Materials and preparation: None

Activity: In this game people are trying not to win or to lose. The leader starts by dividing the group into pairs. Each pair finds a space in the room away from the others. They stand side by side, hips touching. They then introduce themselves to their partner by saying: "My name is … and I'm going to push you over." Each person pushes their partner from the hip as hard as they can, but they must not push them over. They must be aware of their partner's strength and push just enough so as not to push them over. After 30 seconds, they all change partners and repeat the process, until they have all met and pushed each other.

Variation: Swap hips.

Closure: The leader talks with the group about how they feel.

Rhythm of the name

Aim: Ice breaking, getting to know each other

Time: 10 minutes

Materials and preparation: None

Activity: The leader asks the group to form a circle. One person then goes into the middle, says their name and executes any kind of movement or rhythm, as strange or as normal as they want. The whole group repeat the name and the rhythm in unison. The individual then returns to the edge of the circle and someone else goes into the middle and follows the same procedure. The game stops when everyone has had a go.

Variation: As above, but sitting down.

Closure: The leader asks the group how they feel.

It's up to you

Aim: Ice breaking, creativity, introductions

Time: 10 minutes

Materials and preparation: None

Activity: The leader asks the group to form a circle. Participants are told that they are about to introduce themselves to the group, but they must not speak their names and they must not copy the way someone else has introduced themselves: they must find some other way of communicating their names to the group. For example, they may sing their name, grunt their name, write out their name, act out their name, tap out their name and so on. When the name has been communicated, the whole group then say the name and copy the way it was communicated in unison. Members take it in turn to communicate their own name until everyone has had a go.

Variation: Make a song of everyone's name.

Closure: The leader goes through everyone's names and asks people how they feel.

Closures

Often when we run a group we give more attention to warming up a group than on its ending or cooling down. It is important to remember that the type of energy generated in a group is different from the energy of the everyday world and therefore special consideration needs to be given to the transition from the group to the outside world. We could say that group members are 'in role' as members of the group and need to 'derole' from the group so they can return themselves to their role in society.

Sudden endings of any kind are always a shock and, particularly in groupwork, can mitigate against all that has been learnt. An appropriate ending maximizes the learning and change that have taken place in the group; it also acts as a model for everyday life. For example, it may help the person who has been emotionally scarred by repeated walk-outs, with door slamming by parents, to learn how to make an ending.

Endings in our day-to-day life are a transition from one state to another, such as school and home, work and holiday and so on. Endings that are final, such as death, divorce or miscarriage and so on, will influence our response to endings in groups. *Some group members may well find it difficult to deal with the closure process and may attempt to leave the room during the ending process.* (See the reference to transitional groups on p4.)

Reviewing the group 1

Aim: Closure

Time: 5 minutes

Materials and preparation: None

Activity: Ask the members to stand in a circle, to have a stretch and then close their eyes. Invite them to think back to the beginning of the group and how they felt when they arrived. They should then think through all the different things that they have done in the group and how they felt about them. Finally, they should all think of one positive thing that they take away with them. Participants open their eyes and do one last stretch.

Variations: As above, but sitting back to back.
As above, but lying down.

Closure: People say goodbye to each other.

Reviewing the group 2

Aim: Closure

Time: 5 minutes

Materials and preparation: None

Activity: As in 'Reviewing the group 1', but invite people to picture the group as if it were a film or video. In their minds they should run through all the things that have happened in the session and then *allow it to have an ending*. The group leader should ask participants, "What has the group given you to take away and think about?" Members then open their eyes and do one final stretch.

Variations: As above, but standing back to back.
As above, but standing linked in a chain.

Closure: People say goodbye to each other.

Reviewing the group 3

Aim: Closure

Time: 10 minutes

Materials and preparation: None

Activity: The group leader should ask everyone to lie down on their backs with their hands by their sides and their eyes closed. The leader then talks the group through what they have done in that session, then asks everyone to think of one positive thing that happened in the group. How do they feel about this thing? The leader then asks participants to try and concentrate on that *feeling*, rather than the thing itself. People may get up in their own time and open their eyes.

Closure: People smile at each other and wave goodbye.

Retelling the group 1

Aim: Closure

Time: 15 minutes

Materials and preparation: None

Activity: The group leader should invite everyone to stand in a circle and ask them to remember all the things they have done in the group. Then, each contributing in turn, they retell it all as a short story. (No one person can speak for more than three sentences.)

Closure: The leader asks people how they feel.

Retelling the group 2

Aim: Closure

Time: 15 minutes

Materials and preparation: None

Activity: The group leader should invite everyone to stand in a circle and ask them to remember all the things they have done in the group. Then, each contributing in turn, they retell it all as a short mime. (Each mime should last about a minute.)

Closure: The leader talks with the group about how they feel.

Retelling the group 3

Aim: Closure

Time: 15 minutes

Materials and preparation: None

Activity: The group leader should invite everyone to stand in a circle and ask them to remember all the things they have done in the group. Then, each contributing in turn, they retell it all as a short story and should finish by saying what they would like to happen in the next session.

Closure: The leader talks with the group about how they feel.

Retelling the group 4

Aim: Closure

Time: 15 minutes

Materials and preparation: None

Activity: The group leader should invite everyone to stand in a circle and ask them to remember all the things they have done in the group. Then, each contributing in turn, they retell it all as a short story. The story should take an agreed form, such as a mystery, a whodunit or a thriller.

Closure: The leader talks with the group about how they feel.

Closing to music

Aim: Closure

Time: 5–10 minutes

Materials and preparation: Some prerecorded music and a player

Activity: Some prerecorded music is played while the group stretch out. They are then asked to lie on their backs with their arms by their sides and to think about the positive things that have happened in the session for them. While this is happening, the group leader should very slowly turn down the music until it is barely audible. Participants are invited to get up in their own time, taking care not to get up too quickly.

Variation: Suggest that different people bring in music to close to each week.

Closure: The leader talks with the group about how they feel.

Business meeting closure

Aim: Closure

Time: 15 minutes

Materials and preparation: Tape recorder and taped music

Activity: Everyone sits in a circle. They elect a member to the chair and discuss through the chair whether the group has fulfilled all its aims and objectives for the session and, if not, why not. The leader reminds members of the group rules (if appropriate) and talks about the plan for the next week. The leader talks about who is not at the session and whether the group needs to know why. (For example, do we need to send a card to a member who is in hospital?)

Closure: The leader talks with the group about how they feel.

Fill that space

Aim: Closure

Time: 5 minutes

Materials and preparation: None

Activity: Participants are asked to walk in slow motion around the room, filling up any space that they see. They must jump slowly (not easy) into a space when they see it but not stay there, keeping on moving around the room. They must be aware of each other and the space, not bumping into each other or the walls. The leader lets this go on for a little while and then shouts out, "Stop!" All the participants must freeze where they are. The idea is that they should all be spread around the whole floor, spaced equally. The leader could at this point make them aware of any empty spaces left around the room. Repeat this several times.

Variation: I use a variation of this game as a warm-up: basically the same game, speeded up. This is useful to know when devising closures; one can often take a warm-up, slow it right down and it becomes an excellent closure.

Closure: Participants share their feelings with the group.

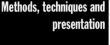

Games and exercises for exploring difficulties

Drama is used as a therapeutic medium by many people and is indeed the core of the work of such people as psychodramatists and dramatherapists. Some drama techniques can be useful and applicable in any groupwork, and examples will be found in the activities that follow.

Chapter 4 discussed areas that can cause problems and it suggested training and pre-planning that could overcome some of these. The games and exercises that follow are for exploring difficulties and getting the best out of our groups when we are actually in session.

Image of the group

Aim: Discovering and uncovering problems in the group

Time: 60 minutes

Materials and preparation: None

Activity:

This exercise can be used at any time but is particularly useful when the leader feels that the group members are not working well together. It is also a good way of seeing how each participant sees the group as a whole. Sometimes people might not want to participate in a group, or want to prevaricate, or just feel plain stubborn.

The group leader should invite volunteers to build an image of the group, continually consulting the group as to progress, adding elements or taking away those that are non-essential. Eventually an image is created and the group leader reminds everyone that they are part of the image. Even those people who refused to participate are part of the overall image because they are taking roles of people who are refusing to participate. So within the room there will be one giant image with a nucleus of people on the inside and people on the outside who are refusing to participate or maybe are just 'happy watching'. Now the leader tells those people who are happy with their positions in the nucleus to stay there and those that are unhappy with their positions in the nucleus to go and sit down. The group leader should also tell those that are not participating or are just watching that, if they feel uncomfortable with their positions, they may either join the nucleus or go and sit down. After all these movements have been done, the group leader asks the participants to come out of the image and to go back in wherever they want (not in a position that has been imposed on them). This final image should show you whether the group is able to work together harmoniously, what transformations may be needed and what hidden grievances people may be holding.

Closure:

The leader talks to the group about these images: how did they make them feel? Are the divisions too great?

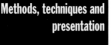

Revelations 1

Aim: Exploring relationships within the group, dealing with change

Time: 100 minutes (minimum)

Materials and preparation: The group should be thoroughly warmed up

Activity: The group decides on which relationship to explore: one that is pertinent to the group. The group leader should ask everyone to find a partner and tell them to decide who is playing what, how they usually greet each other and interact, and so on.

Simultaneously each pair meets and begins an improvisation on how they greet each other and what they might normally say. Give them a few minutes to get to know their characters and then bring them all into a circle. Tell everybody to remember how and where they met and what was said. Ask the first couple to go into the centre of the circle and show everybody details of their meeting. After a few minutes, the group leader should say, "One of you make a revelation of great importance that has the potential to change your relationship." (Examples are "I'm pregnant", "I've joined a new group", "I'm having an affair with your wife", "I'm going away", and so on.) The other person should react in the way they feel their character would react in real life. After a few more minutes, the group leader should tell the other person to make an important revelation. Their partner should react in the way they feel their character would. How is their relationship now? The group leader should now tell one of them that they have to leave. The couple should improvise their parting. Will they ever see each other again? The group leader should thank the couple and ask them to sit down. Each pair in turn is asked up and should follow the same procedure as the first.

Closure: How did this game make people feel? What was the range of revelations and how did people react? Why did people react in certain ways? How many stereotypes did we see?

Revelations 2

Aim: Searching for new paths

Time: 40 minutes

Materials and preparation: The group should have played 'Revelations 1'

Activity: Ask the group to pick several of the improvisations from 'Revelations 1' to be repeated; they should try to pick ones that were highly charged. Take the first improvisation up to the point of the reaction to the first revelation and then shout, "Stop!" Ask if anyone would like to show a possible different reaction. Replay the improvisation with as many different reactions as people want to offer, then do the same thing with the second revelation and finally with the parting. Repeat all this with several more chosen improvisations.

Closure: The leader talks with the group about how this activity made them feel. How many ways of reacting to a situation are there? How did reactions change the relationship?

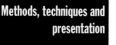

The machine of the group

Aim: Exploring how group members feel about the group

Time: 20 minutes

Materials and preparation: None

Activity:

The leader explains that the participants are going to make a machine that will represent the whole group. It starts with the first person going into the centre of the space and imagining they are *a moving part* of a very complicated machine, a machine of their own choice, as long as it represents (to them) an important element of the group. This person starts doing a repetitive and mechanical movement with their body and a vocalization to go with it. Everyone else watches and listens for a while. Soon another person gets up and adds their body (another moving part) to the machine. This person adds a different movement and vocalization, keeping in mind the need not only to add to the machine but to make their bit say something which is important to them about the group. They must remember at all times: this is a machine of the group. In turn, each member adds a part to the machine until it is one big, heaving, synchronized mass. At this point the leader takes the place of each of the members in turn, so that that person can come out of the machine and look at it. This game finishes when all members have put themselves in the machine and everyone has seen it working.

Variation:

Split up into groups of five and make lots of mini machines.

Closure:

The leader talks with the group about how they feel. What was the machine like? How did all the parts complement each other? What difficulties did the machine have? Did the machine break down? What different things were represented in the machine and how do they relate to the group?

Forum theatre 1

Aim: Improvisation, group transaction and exploring problems within the group

Time: 60 minutes (minimum)

Materials and preparation: Group warm-up

Activity: Decide on a topic that the group wish to explore (such as anger in the group, people not turning up, difficulties in communication and so on). Split the group into two-thirds the audience and one-third actors. The actors are going to improvise for the audience a very short scene on the chosen topic. Give the actors five minutes to talk about the chosen topic and who is going to play what in the scene. (For example, if the subject of the group not working well was chosen, the actors will have to show a scene where individuals are at odds with one another.) After the five minutes, ask the actors to come and perform their scene, which should be two or three minutes long. When the scene is finished, ask the audience to comment on the content of the piece (not the acting). Have the group suffered the same or similar problems?

After a few minutes of discussion, ask the actors to replay the scene. This time the audience have a chance to alter the destiny of the characters in the play. They are told that, whenever they see a chance to make the situation better, they should shout, "Stop!" and the actors will freeze in their positions. The person who shouts 'stop' is then coaxed out of their seat into the playing area, and asked to show what they would have done in that particular situation. So this person takes the place of the actor who was in the most difficulty in the performance and acts out what they would have done. The other actors have to improvise around this new actor and should be thinking, "Does this character's new actions make any difference to my character?" If they do, then they must change, as they would in real life. Once the new way has been tried, other people are invited to show what they would do. Do this as many times as is required. Remember that there are no 'better' ways, there are just 'different' ways. What is right for one person is not necessarily right for another.

Closure: At the end of the session, talk to the group about how this exercise made them feel. What did they see? How many different solutions were offered? Why did one work and another not work so well? Can they use what they have discovered in sorting out the problems from which the group suffer? In what way?

Forum theatre 2

Aim: Improvisation, group transaction and exploring problems within the group

Time: 120 minutes (minimum)

Materials and preparation: The group should be thoroughly warmed up

Activity:

Decide on two topics that the group wish to explore (they should be issues that the group have difficulty in dealing with or issues which stop the group from working). Split the group in half, with each sub-group having one of the topics, around which they are to devise a scene. They should have sufficient time to rehearse the scene – it is recommended that 30 to 60 minutes be allowed for this. After rehearsal, the two sub-groups take it in turns to perform their pieces. When both performances have been watched the whole group should spend some time discussing what they saw. Have the issues been performed correctly? Did characters behave as they do when they are in the group?

After discussion and a break, the leader should encourage the sub-groups to spend another 30 minutes refining their pieces, taking into account what has been raised in the discussion. The groups are now ready for the forum.

This time, before the first sub-group start their scene, those watching are invited to stop the play whenever they see a character or the sub-group as a whole in some kind of difficulty. The person who stopped the play is encouraged to take the place of the actor who was in difficulty and show a possible way out of this. The group leader should encourage all kinds of interventions: "Try anything – see if it works." All kinds of bizarre attempts might show a way to overcome a difficulty that has previously been hidden. When taking over an actor's role, the person intervening should tell the other actors where to restart the play. As this new person will be deviating from the planned performance, the actors must improvise around the changes.

It is important that the actors stay true to their characters and do not make it too easy for the newcomer but, having said this, they should also allow for changes in their characters if what the newcomer does would (in the real life of the group) change their character's actions. After each intervention, the leader should check with the audience whether they thought characters played as they would have done if it had been a real-life situation. Encourage other audience members to show different ways of overcoming the difficulty. Repeat this process until the end of the scene. Now the groups swap over and the forum process is repeated.

This exercise is very flexible indeed. For example, it could go on for three hours in a single day's workshop or last three weeks in a long-running workshop (or even longer). Find out how the group feel at the end of each session. Are everyone's views being represented? Are the solutions found real solutions: that is, can they be transferred to reality? If people manage to overcome difficulties in a forum theatre setting, they could also overcome them within the real life of the group.

Closure: Actors should symbolically mark the leaving of their characters and return to themselves. The leader talks with the group about what has come up in this session and how group members feel. Can we transfer solutions back to the reality of the group?

Blind exploration

Aim: Breaking down our visual prejudices
Time: 10 minutes
Materials and preparation: Blindfolds (optional); the group should be warmed up

Activity: The leader instructs everyone to close their eyes or to put on blindfolds. They then walk slowly round the space with their hands out in front of them. When they come across someone else each should (without talking) explore the other's face with their hands, feeling the shape of the face, cheeks, nose, lips, head, ears, length of hair and so on. In this way each should form a picture in their mind of the other. After a minute, they open their eyes and talk to each other about the experience. The leader should let this exercise go on for as long as is felt appropriate.

NB This game is not suitable for 12 to 17-year-olds.

Variation: Explore hands.

Closure: The leader talks with the group about how they feel.

Role-play 1

Aim: Exploring how others feel

Time: 5 minutes

Materials and preparation: None

Activity: The leader asks the group to form a circle and asks those in the group that have difficulty interacting with each other to step into the centre. A typical situation is then chosen where these people are likely to have difficulties with each other. Very often it could be some kind of confrontation, such as asking someone to stop doing something. This scenario is then enacted in front of the group, with people in the centre of the circle taking on the roles of those with whom they are having difficulty. In this enactment people improvise their new character; for example, if there are two people, they will be playing each other's roles. The group leader should let this go on for as long as is appropriate, while making sure that the actors know that what they are doing is role-playing and not real life.

Variation: Improvise possible solutions. Do they work?

Closure: The leader talks to the actors about how they feel. What was it like being presented with yourself? Were the characterizations realistic? What did the group feel watching it? Ask the actors to shake hands and leave behind the characters they have just played in the circle.

Role-play 2

Aim: Exploring how the group functions

Time: 60 minutes

Materials and preparation: Everyone's name should be written on a piece of paper and put into a hat

Activity: This game is very intensive and needs the co-operation of those involved. The leader needs to explain that this is an experiment, so people should not worry about getting anything wrong because nothing they do will be wrong. Each member is instructed to take a piece of paper from the hat; if they pull out their own name they should put it back and pull out another. Thus everyone should have the name of another group member. Members should now play the character on the paper; they should not make fun of it (this is something that the leader should watch out for) but should play it seriously as they see it. The group should now choose a topic that they have previously had difficulty exploring and then work on it in their new characters. After some time, the leader should call an end to the activity.

Closure: Everyone closes their eyes and imagines their character walking away from them and turning a corner, waving goodbye. Each group member should now hug or shake the hand of the person they played. The leader talks with the group about how they feel. What did this exercise bring up that had not been seen before? Can any new perspectives be seen?

Hot seat transfer

Aim: Seeing yourself through others' eyes, group exploration

Time: 30 minutes

Materials and preparation: A chair

Activity: The leader organizes the group into a semi-circle, with everyone sitting down. A chair is placed facing the group and each member in turn sits on the chair, faces the group and tells them their name, what interests them or what work they do, why they are here and what they want to get out of the group. The leader stresses that members should be very attentive to what people say, as they will be working on the material heard later.

After everyone has taken the chair and spoken, the whole exercise is repeated, but this time when people have their turn they do not speak about themselves but about one of the group members they have just heard. Each person should try and mimic the person they are characterizing, right down to the last detail, including what was said, tone of voice, body language and eye contact with group members. It should be remembered that they will be doing this from memory, so they cannot be expected to be word perfect; they are not trying to make fun of that person, but they are trying to repeat what they believe they saw. This game ends when everyone has introduced themselves and when everyone has introduced someone else from the group (as if they were them).

Variation: Someone introduces themselves as above and then someone else comes up and introduces the last person as if they were them, and then introduces themselves, and so on until everyone has had a go at both.

Closure: The leader talks with the group about how they feel. What did it feel like seeing themselves in this way? Were the interpretations true to life? Was anyone unhappy at how they were seen?

Hot seat

Aim:	Opening up, talking in front of the group
Time:	30 minutes
Materials and preparation:	A chair

Activity: The leader organizes the group into a semi-circle with everyone sitting down. A chair is placed facing the group and each member in turn sits on the chair, faces the group, says their name and why they are here. One at a time, group members then ask this person questions about their life. The person on the hot seat can answer in any way they like; if they do not want to answer a question, they can just say, "pass". The objective of the group members asking questions is to be probing, but not to be intimidating or embarrassing. After five minutes, the person on the hot seat is thanked and asked if there is anything else they want to say before they sit down. This continues with the next person following the same procedure and finishes when everyone has had a go.

Variation: The group draws up a list of questions which they can ask.

Closure: The leader talks with the group about how they feel.

The bag

Aim:	Self-expression, creativity, co-operation
Time:	40 minutes
Materials and preparation:	A bag filled with an assortment of objects; these objects can be anything at all, but variation of colour and texture is desirable

Activity: This bag (what a dramatherapist might call a 'Pandora's box of creativity') is placed in front of the leader, who hands out an object to each of the participants. They are asked to go and play with their object in any way they like. After a few moments they are told that, if they want, they can go up to someone else and try to persuade them to swap objects. If people are happy with their objects then they carry on playing with them and do not have to swap them, but if they have been persuaded to swap they start to play with their new object. After a few more minutes, participants are asked to find a partner. Each pair now develops a short scene concerning their two objects. The scene should represent the exploration or sorting out of a group difficulty. After a little time for rehearsal, each pair is asked to perform their scene to the rest of the group.

Closure: How did this exercise make people feel? What stories did these objects bring out of them? Did the objects represent something to them?

Transforming group oppression

Aim: Group transaction, exploring oppression

Time: 90 minutes

Materials and preparation: None

Activity: Ask a volunteer to pick people from the group and to put them into a representation (an image) of an oppressive situation. This oppressive situation should be one that has come from the group – one that the group, or individuals in the group, have suffered. Next the leader should consult the group to see if they can see elements of oppression in the image, elements that are relevant to the group. If they can, it should be left; if they cannot, someone may take it to pieces and rebuild another image of oppression or, if it is nearly right, just tinker at the edges. When an image is found that the whole group finds acceptable, this should be used. What is oppressive for one person is not necessarily so for another and the group may have to set up a series of images to represent everyone's view.

Once there is an image (or a series of images) of oppression that everyone agrees with, ask the group to construct the 'ideal' image, where all the oppression has been taken out and all the characters in the image have reached a state of perfect equilibrium with each other. Once this is done, the two images are placed side by side. What do group members see? What changes have occurred? Ask members in turn to show what characters might have done to get from being oppressed to not being oppressed.

Variation: Use the activity to explore difficulties that the group may have in working together: make an image of the difficulties and explore them.

Closure: How do the images feel? Are these real solutions or could they not happen in real life? Why? Can these solutions be transferred to the group to sort out group difficulties, misunderstandings and so on? Everyone shares with the group how they feel.

Using Shakespeare

Aim: Widening perception and insight; change and experimentation; understanding Shakespeare

Time: 60 minutes (minimum)

Materials and preparation: The group should be warmed up vocally and physically; they will have played some drama games; they will need a Shakespearean text to work with

Activity: The group leader will first of all have to have a feel for the 'theme' that is running through the group: why is the group meeting? The leader should pick a text from a Shakespeare play that contains issues the group are dealing with. How is the play going to help them explore the subject without making group members feel exposed? Remember that, thanks to dramatic distance, the play will contain everyone's story, so everyone will be able to look at what is appropriate to their lives and how they interact with those around them. If it is not possible for the group to have seen the play previously, the group leader should give as detailed a summary as possible of the play to the group, reading out certain sections, or getting group members to read certain roles. The group are then ready to embark on their experimentation.

Divide the group into pairs and get each pair to do repeated improvisations around a few lines chosen from the play. Encourage them to immerse themselves in their characters and the complex relationship that these two characters have. Exploring these improvisations will allow participants to make their own journey through the recognition of what is in themselves. Each of the pairs will have different struggles and each will have to use individual skills in this joint endeavour.

Variation: The group does not have to stay with Shakespeare. There are many stories that could substitute for or complement Shakespeare and which could in fact be used to follow up work with issues raised in the improvisations. For ideas, dip into any of the following: Gersie A, *Earthtales*, Green Print, London, 1992; Wilhelm R, *I Ching or Book of Changes*, Arkania, London, 1989; Angelou M, *Just Give Me a Cool Drink of Water 'Fore I Die*, Virago, London, 1988.

Closure: The group leader should call a halt at an appropriate moment and bring everyone together to 'derole': everyone should feel distanced from any of the stories that have emerged. At this point, the group can share the 'hot themes' that came out of the improvisations. Why do people feel pressured into doing things they do not want to do? Why have there been problems within the group? What makes relationships work? And so on. Make sure that equal weight is given to everybody's feelings.

Role reversal

Aim: Self-exploration, trust, communication, exploring problems within the group

Time: 40 minutes

Materials and preparation: The group should be thoroughly warmed up

Activity: The leader asks everyone to find a partner (someone they are happy sharing something with), to name themselves A or B and to sit down as far away as possible from the other pairs. A should tell B a story of a difficult relationship they have with someone in the group, telling of typical things that are said and done when A interacts with the other person.

After a few minutes, ask the pairs to improvise a typical encounter, with A playing themselves and B playing the person that A talked about. After a few more minutes they should reverse roles: B should play A, and A should play the character of the person they had the difficulty with. When a few more minutes have passed, ask them to revert back to their original roles and start the improvisation again. Have people changed?

Variation: Now B tells A a story and continues as above.

Closure: The leader brings the group back together and talks to them about how they feel. What was it like watching themselves? Did people modify their behaviour?

Ritual 1

Aim: Movement, creativity, group interaction; preparation for 'Ritual 2'

Time: 30 minutes

Materials and preparation: The group should be warmed up

Activity: The group should pick a topic to ritualize (for example, celebrations). Any topic will do, but it must be one that the whole group agrees upon. Each person invents a rhythm and sound giving their interpretation of the chosen topic. It does not have to be a naturalistic interpretation: it can take any form, including showing people's feelings about the topic. Now that each person has their personal ritual, group members in turn perform each other's.

Closure: The group talk about the various rituals. What were the different interpretations like? How does everyone feel?

Ritual 2

Aim: Building a ritual of repair

Time: 40 minutes

Materials and preparation: The group should be warmed up

Activity: The leader talks with the group about a topic, such as saying goodbye. After some minutes, each person is asked to find a rhythm or a movement that to them represents saying goodbye. When everyone has got their mini rituals, the leader asks them to find a partner and to share their rituals with each other. After a little while, the leader asks the pairs to try and incorporate their two rituals in one. Eventually the group leader should bring the group back together and, each pair in turn, they can perform their rituals to the rest of the group.

Closure: Were any rituals invented that the group think might help group members to say goodbye to each other? Everyone shares with the group how they feel.

Group demystifier 1

Aim: Sharing expectations

Time: 30 minutes

Materials and preparation: Pen and paper for each participant

Activity: Each person should write down, without showing others, *one* expectation they have about the group. Everyone is then brought into a circle and the pieces of paper are folded (anonymity is maintained) and put into a hat. The papers are then mixed up and redistributed. Each person in turn reads out what is on their paper. Members talk about what they have heard. Do they have the same expectations? If there are differences, why is this, and are they all compatible?

Closure: The leader talks with the group about keeping a groupwork diary for personal reference and for sharing with the group at appropriate times.

Group demystifier 2

Aim: Sharing likes and dislikes

Time: 30 minutes

Materials and preparation: Pen and paper for each participant

Activity: Each person should write down, without showing others, *one* thing they would like to be. Everyone is then brought into a circle and the pieces of paper are folded (anonymity is maintained) and put in a hat. The papers are then mixed up and redistributed. Each person in turn reads out what is on their paper. Members talk about what they have heard. Do they have the same likes? What are the differences? Can everyone's likes be brought into the group process (and would this be appropriate)?

Closure: The leader talks with the group about keeping a groupwork diary for personal reference and for sharing with the group at appropriate times.

Group demystifier 3

Aim: Sharing views of the group

Time: 30 minutes

Materials and preparation: Pen and paper for each participant

Activity: Each person should draw or write down, without showing others, a picture or a phrase representing how they see the group at the moment. Everyone is then brought into a circle and the pieces of paper are folded (anonymity is maintained) and put in a hat. The papers are then mixed up and redistributed. Each person in turn reads out what is on their paper. Members talk about what they have heard. How many different pictures or phrases have been shown? Can some of the pictures or phrases be linked up with each other? What do all these tell us about the present state of the group? Can things be improved? Do they want to make things different?

Closure: The leader talks with the group about keeping a groupwork diary for personal reference and for sharing with the group at appropriate times.

Group demystifier 4

Aim: Sharing memories of the group process

Time: 30 minutes

Materials and preparation: Pen and paper for each participant

Activity: Each person should write down, without showing others, *one* sentence describing how they thought the group was an hour ago, last session or when the group first met. Everyone is then brought into a circle and the pieces of paper are folded (anonymity is maintained) and put in a hat. The papers are then mixed up and redistributed. Each person in turn reads out what is on their paper. Members talk about the different perceptions. Do people have the same ideas? What changes have taken place?

Closure: The leader talks with the group about keeping a groupwork diary for personal reference and for sharing with the group at appropriate times.

Metaphor of the group

Aim: Sharing group perceptions and bringing people's ideas of the group together in a constructive manner

Time: 30 minutes

Materials and preparation: None

Activity: The leader should bring the group into a circle and ask members in turn to answer the question, "If this group was a fruit, what would it be?" When all the suggestions have been made, the group discusses all the different fruits. Why have particular fruits been chosen?

Variation: If this group was a machine, what would it be?

Closure: What fruits have been suggested? Is it possible to make a fruit salad that everyone would enjoy?

Teambuilding 1

Aim: Discovering positive and negative images of a team; encouraging tolerance and awareness

Time: 30 minutes

Materials and preparation: Activity suitable for six people; pens and paper (optional)

Activity: This exercise is particularly useful when communication within an existing team has broken down and the group leader is helping the group discover new ways of relating to each other. The group leader invites each person to think of an image or metaphor of the way they thought of the group previously. The image can be written down or given orally. Members must be given time to think of the image first, before sharing – otherwise some will compete. Members then share each other's perceptions.

This exercise is particularly useful for the leader; if, for example, a high proportion of the group saw the group as a derelict crane, this would tell the leader much! If everyone in the group has a different metaphor, the group represents a learning experience through which to understand each other's perspectives.

Closure: The group share ways in which they would like to change the metaphor.

Teambuilding 2

Aim: Discovering positive and negative images of a team; encouraging tolerance and awareness; unifying group ideas

Time: 30 minutes

Materials and preparation: Activity suitable for six people; pens and paper (optional)

Activity: This exercise is particularly useful when communication within an existing team has broken down and the group leader is helping the group discover new ways of relating to each other. The group leader invites each person to think of an image or metaphor of the way they thought of the group previously. The image can be written down or given orally. Members must be given time to think of the image first, before sharing – otherwise some will compete. Members then share each other's perceptions. Through discussion, see if the group can bring all the metaphors together as a single whole. They can be joined or manipulated to fit only with everyone's general agreement.

Closure: Did the group manage to unify their metaphors? What did it take?

Teambuilding 3

Aim: Discovering positive and negative images of a team

Time: 30 minutes

Materials and preparation: Activity suitable for six people; pen and paper for each participant

Activity: This exercise is particularly useful when communication within an existing team has broken down and the group leader is helping the group discover new ways of relating to each other. The group leader invites each person to think of an image or metaphor of the way they thought of the group previously. Members must be given time to think of the image first, before sharing – otherwise some will compete. Now each person should draw their image on a piece of paper.

When the drawings are finished (allow three minutes) bring them all into the centre and try to fit them together like a jigsaw. Is this possible? What does the final picture tell us?

Closure: How do people feel about the final picture?

Teambuilding 4

Aim: Discovering positive and negative images of a team

Time: 30 minutes

Materials and preparation: Activity suitable for six people; paint and brushes for all participants, one large piece of paper

Activity: This exercise is particularly useful when communication within an existing team has broken down and the group leader is helping the group discover new ways of relating to each other. The group leader invites each person to think of an image or metaphor of the way they thought of the group previously. Members must be given time to think of the image first, before sharing – otherwise some will compete.

Together the group paint their metaphor on the large piece of paper. When they have finished, they talk about the image. What does it tell them? What are the predominant feelings?

Closure: The leader talks about the complete image and how individual efforts made up the whole. Are they complementary?

Teambuilding 5

Aim: Discovering positive and negative images of a team

Time: 60 minutes

Materials and preparation: Activity suitable for six people; pens and paper (optional)

Activity: This exercise is particularly useful when communication within an existing team has broken down and the group leader is helping the group discover new ways of relating to each other. The group leader invites each person to think of an image or metaphor of the way they thought of the group previously. The image can be written down or given orally. Members must be given time to think of the image first, before sharing – otherwise some will compete.

Using all the metaphors, the group create a mini drama or scene using improvisation. The leader should make sure that all the metaphors are incorporated.

Closure: The leader should make sure members are 'deroled' and then talk about the improvisation. What came out of the show? Members share with the group how they feel.

Teambuilding 6

Aim: Discovering positive and negative images of a team; stretching and movement

Time: 45 minutes

Materials and preparation: Activity suitable for six people; pens and paper (optional)

Activity: This exercise is particularly useful when communication within an existing team has broken down and the group leader is helping the group discover new ways of relating to each other. The group leader invites each person to think of an image or metaphor of the way they thought of the group previously. The image can be written down or given orally. Members must be given time to think of the image first, before sharing – otherwise some will compete. Using all the metaphors, the group are encouraged to create a dance of the group. This can be done by the group as a whole or people can devise individual steps from their own metaphors, which are then brought together into a whole dance or a sequence of dances.

Closure: The leader talks with the group about how they feel.

Do create a song and dance about it

Aim: Discovering positive and negative images of the group; unifying the group

Time: 60 minutes

Materials and preparation: None

Activity: The group leader invites members to think up a simile of the group ('The group is like a …'). When everyone has thought up their similes, ask them to find a partner with whom to share them. Each pair should then use their similes to create a ritual, such as saying the similes in a rhythm. They perform these rituals to the rest of the group. Once all the rituals have been performed, the group try to unify them into one group chant or movement.

Closure: The leader talks with the group about how they feel.

Whose decision is it anyway?

Aim: Making decisions in a group activity

Time: 20–40 minutes

Materials and preparation: None

Activity: The leader and group members decide on a group activity such as a game, a problem to solve or a journey to make. Then the leader says, "We do not know how to do this, so we must decide as a group the rules and the process we must go through." Each person in turn then suggests one thing that will help achieve the performance of the group activity. As each suggestion is made, the group as a whole does the thing suggested. The game finishes when each person has verbalized at least one decision.

Closure: Did the group complete the activity? How did the group reach its decisions? Were there any leaders? Were things achieved co-operatively? The leader talks with the group about how they feel.

Nature

Aim: Expressing how we feel

Time: 15 minutes

Materials and preparation: None

Activity: The leader points out that we use metaphors of nature to describe many things in life such as 'breaking the ice', 'stuck in the mud' or 'no light at the end of the tunnel'. Each group member is then invited to describe how they are feeling, using a metaphor from nature (they can make these up themselves). When the group has heard all the metaphors, they face a choice: either to keep their own metaphors or to take someone else's if they feel it describes better how they feel, or if it describes how they would like to feel.

The group start a chant, each member chanting their metaphor, quietly at first, then gradually getting louder and louder.

Closure: The leader talks with the group about the metaphors. Did they change them? If so why? How did they feel when they had changed?

The following 'blind' activities are good warm-ups for games later in this section. They also help to build trust within the group and develop other senses, which in turn leads to confidence and group bonding and building.

Blind sound

Aim: To listen and interpret what we hear; warm-up

Time: 20 minutes

Materials and preparation: None

Activity: The leader asks the group to get into twos, each pair to name themselves A or B. A should close their eyes and listen while B makes a distinct, constant and repetitive sound. Give A a minute to listen to this sound. Then ask B to move about the space, repeating the same noise. A, with eyes closed, must follow B around the space, using their partner's sound as a guide. If B stops making the sound then A must stop moving. B must guide A, using the sound only, around the space, being careful not to let A bump into walls or other people. After a while, get participants to swap their roles so that all the As take the Bs on a journey around the space.

Closure: How did members feel while blind? Were they confused by the sounds from other pairs? Did anyone end up following another person's sound? What kind of sound did they feel they were following (that is, did they imagine it was a human voice or did they imagine it was something else)?

Blind catch

Aim: Exploring the group, warm-up, fun

Time: 20 minutes

Materials and preparation: None

Activity: The leader asks everyone to close their eyes and fold their arms in front of them with their hands covering their elbows. They then begin to move around the space slowly, without talking. When they meet people they should greet them without words and move on. After a while the group leader suggests several tasks for each person to undertake, still with their eyes closed, using touch to explore. For example, they have to find people the same height as them and 'stick' to them. After some time, the groups that have formed may open their eyes and check their choices.
Other tasks, performed in the same way, might involve: finding people with the same length of hair; with a similar face; or wearing shoes similar to their own.

Closure: The leader talks with the group about how they feel after playing this game.

Blind return

Aim: Stimulating several senses, contact, movement, warm-up

Time: 20 minutes

Materials and preparation: None

Activity:

Part 1

Everyone is asked to fix their gaze on any place in the room. They then close their eyes, stretch their arms out in front of them and walk slowly to the place they had located. They must not open their eyes (even if they bump into other people) until they feel that the place has been reached. Do this three times. How close did people get?

Part 2

The leader asks everyone to find a partner and hug them. In mid-embrace they must close their eyes, release from the hug, walk backwards a pre-arranged number of steps and then return to hug their partner. Do this three times. Did people end up hugging the right partners?

Part 3

The leader asks everyone to find a different partner and shake their hands. In mid-handshake they must close their eyes, release from the shake, walk backwards a pre-arranged number of steps and then return for another handshake with their partner. Do this three times. Did they end up shaking hands with the right partners?

Closure: At the end of the game, the leader asks the group how this game made them feel.

Blind slalom

Aim: Movement, concentration, warm-up

Time: 20 minutes

Materials and preparation: None

Activity: Five people position themselves in a line, a metre apart, in the centre of the space. The rest of the group, one by one, must position themselves at one end of the line and then in turn slalom (with eyes closed) around the five, going no faster than walking pace.

Closure: The leader talks to the group about how this game made them feel.

Not waving but drowning

Aim: Communication, understanding body language

Time: 10 minutes

Materials and preparation: None

Activity: The group should sit in a large circle. Each person in turn is invited into the centre of the circle, where they wave to the others in any way they like, but without speaking. The rest of the group then suggest why they were waving. Were they saying 'hello', 'goodbye', 'help!', 'I am stuck', 'it's that way' or what?

Closure: The leader talks with the group about gestures having different meanings. Can they always tell what people are communicating to them? How does the group feel?

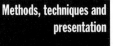

Does she take sugar? 1

Aim: Exploring lack of communication; warm-up for 'Does she take sugar? 2'

Time: 25 minutes

Materials and preparation: One chair for each group of three people

Activity: The group divides into threes, with individuals called A, B or C. Each group should then find a space away from the other groups, taking a chair with them. The As sit in the chair, the Bs stand behind them holding the top of the chair as if pushing them (imagining that it is a wheelchair) and the Cs start up a conversation with the Bs.

During the conversation B and C should make enquiries about A but never address A directly. B and C avoid talking *to* A the whole time but talk *about* them instead. After several minutes, they all swap round and do the same again. Finally, they swap round a third time, so that each person has had a go in the chair.

Closure: The leader brings the whole group back together and talks about the experience. What was it like being talked about?
Group members shake hands or hug each other.

Does she take sugar? 2

Aim: Exploring lack of communication and what it takes to be noticed

Time: 40 minutes

Materials and preparation: The group should have played 'Does she take sugar? 1'; one chair for each group of three people

Activity: Follow the same guidelines as in the previous game, but this time A should try and get themselves included in the conversation in any way they like. B and C should carry on excluding them at first, but after a while they may (if they have been persuaded enough) start to include them in their dialogue directly.

Closure: After a group hug or handshake, the leader talks to the group about how they felt playing this exercise. What was it like to be ignored? How did A grab the attention of B and C? How did B and C feel when they were forced to talk to A?

Ears, eyes and mouth 1

Aim: Exploring loss of the senses, warm-up for 'Ears, eyes and mouth 2'

Time: 25 minutes

Materials and preparation: Pen and paper (optional)

Activity: The group split into threes. Within each group of three, one person is deaf, one person is blind and one person is mute. Keeping to these strict guidelines, they should complete a task such as getting from one side of the room to another without bumping into anyone, or writing a poem. After a few minutes, members swap over and take on another task; they repeat this a third time so that each person has had a go at each role.

Closure: The leader talks with the group about how they felt playing this game. What difficulties did they encounter? How did they overcome difficulties?

Ears, eyes and mouth 2

Aim: Exploring loss of senses, adaptation and co-operation

Time: 30–40 minutes

Materials and preparation: The group should have played 'Ears, eyes and mouth 1'

Activity: This game is very difficult and careful co-operation is needed between players. It is similar to the last game but there is more loss of sense. The group split into threes. Within each group of three, one person can hear, one person can see and one person can speak. See what kind of tasks the groups can complete. Is there room for cross-group co-operation?

Closure: The leader brings the whole group back together and talks with them about how they feel. What kinds of activities did they manage? How difficult was it? To lose one sense is difficult but to lose two can be devastating: how did they cope with this?

Survival

Aim: Problem solving, group decision making

Time: 30–40 minutes

Materials and preparation: Obstacles such as chairs, tables and mats (optional)

Activity: Members form groups of four. Each group is to imagine that they have been parachuted into a remote area and they must find their way through a forest, cross a deep river, scale a steep rockface and cross some quicksand. Apart from the parachutes, they can only take one thing with them. Groups must first decide what this one thing is they are taking with them and then they start on their journey. They should plan and play this game as if it were happening in real life.

Closure: The leader talks to the group about how they feel. What was the one thing they took on their journey? How did they overcome the obstacles? Were the parachutes useful? How did the groups make decisions?

Crosswords 1

Aim: Exploring lack of understanding

Time: 10 minutes

Materials and preparation: None

Activity: The group divide into pairs. One person is a lodger and the other is the landlord. Through talking, the landlord should try and make the lodger pay the rent and the lodger should try to avoid paying at all costs. The lodger makes excuses and the landlord demands the rent. The leader lets this go on for a few minutes and then pairs swap over.

Closure: The leader brings the whole group back together and they talk about how they feel.

Crosswords 2

Aim: Working with disruption; flexibility

Time: 20 minutes

Materials and preparation: None

Activity: The leader invites the group to stand in a square. The people in the sides facing each other should now combine so that there are now two groups. Each group is asked to choose a problem (any problem) and decide how they would, as a group, solve it. For example, a group could choose the problem of trying to create a coherent group story, or the problem of taking a group photograph or picture. The group would then try to complete the said task; in the latter case, the group would need to find a camera and film, or pen, paper and someone who can draw. How should they pose? Who stands at the front and why? Who makes decisions? If everyone is in the picture, then who will take the photo? And so on.

When this has all been agreed, the group leader should take one person from each group and then tell the groups to try and complete their task. After a little while, the leader asks both the people that were taken out of their groups to go back to their group and say to one of the members: "I want to have a word with you." This person should then have several words with them – telling them off for something (made up) and generally distracting them from their work. In the above example, they could try and re-arrange the posing positions for the picture, or tell people that they do not know how to operate a camera, or tell the group a totally irrelevant story, and so on.

Closure: The group leader should then call the whole group back together. They talk about the problems they were tackling. Did they manage to complete them? What was it like having the first distraction of someone being removed from their group? What was it like with the second distraction of the interruption? If either group still completed their task, how did they manage it? Did people work co-operatively?

The Greeks have a word for it

Aim: Finding unconventional solutions, lying convincingly

Time: 30 minutes

Materials and preparation: None

Activity: The whole group think about various problems and come up with enough problems to provide one for every four people in the group. Then they form groups of four and each group is given one problem to explore. Each group of four now split into pairs: one pair comes up with a solution that is nonsense and the other pair thinks how to make the problem more difficult, with a nonsensical question. The pairs are then brought back together so that they may try and convince each other of their solution or the worsening problem.

After a while, the whole group is brought back together for each pair to perform their argument.

Closure: The leader talks with the group about the various arguments. Were they so outrageous? Could any of the solutions, slightly modified, be a real solution? How did people feel playing this game?

It's on the tip of my tongue

Aim: Helping out and telling stories

Time: 30 minutes

Materials and preparation: None

Activity: The leader invites the group to get into pairs, identifying themselves as A and B. A starts a sentence to B: "I want to tell you about … about …" With A not being able to finish the sentence, B should come in with a suggestion as to what A wanted to say. Whatever it is, A must say, "Yes, that's right … I … I …" Again A cannot say what it was they were going to say about the thing that they forgot in the first place. So B comes up with another suggestion, which again A agrees with. Again A cannot remember what to say next, so B chips in. This goes on until B has ended up telling the whole story. For example:

A   I want to tell you about … about …

B   A fish?

A   Yes, that's right. Well this fish … um … um …

B   What? Swam about in the deepest parts of the ocean?

A   Yes. Well, its name was … um … its name was … um …

B   Derrick?

A   Yes. Anyway, Derrick the fish was … um … was … um …

B   Was knocked out after it hit a rock?

A   Yes, that's right, and then … um … then it … um …

B   Was eaten for dinner with a plate of chips?

And so on.

After the stories have been told, the pairs swap over and do the same again.

Closure: The leader brings the group back together and they talk about the stories that were told. Were there any common themes? How did people feel playing the game?

In the beginning there was the word

Aim: Creativity, telling stories

Time: 30–40 minutes

Materials and preparation: Pen and paper (optional)

Activity: The individuals in the group are asked to think about the first word they remember learning as a child. When everybody has thought of a word, they are invited in turn to tell the group what it is. The group is then split into pairs and, using all the words that have been suggested, each pair should come up with a story. (A pen and paper might be useful to write the words down.) When the pairs are ready they are invited to reform the group, sitting in a circle. Each pair then tells its story to the group.

Closure: The group talk about the stories. What were the common themes? How far was the imagination stretched? How do people feel?

Words I hate

Aim: Transforming words

Time: 40 minutes

Materials and preparation: Pen and paper

Activity: The group are invited to form a circle and each person is asked to think about words they hate and why they hate them. Each person should choose one of their words and in turn say: "I only have to hear the word [they say the word] and it makes me feel like [they say what they feel when they hear the word]." When everyone has spoken, the group splits up into pairs who are asked to create something (a story, a poem, a statue and so on) using only the words or the feelings suggested in the circle. After five or ten minutes, everyone is brought back together and each pair performs its creation to the rest of the group.

Variation: As above, but using people's favourite words.

Closure: The leader talks with the group about what they have seen. What kinds of creations did they see? How do they now feel about the words they had originally chosen?

My favourite words

Aim:	Transforming words
Time:	30–40 minutes
Materials and preparation:	None

Activity: The group split up into threes; each group of three should find a space in the room as far away as possible from the others. The groups now think about their favourite words. Each person may choose one of their favourite words and 'lend' it to the group, which now has three words. Using only these words they should try and create something they feel is beautiful (a story, a poem, a sculpture, a play and so on).

After a while, everyone is brought back to the centre and forms a circle. Each group is invited to perform their creation to the rest of the people in the circle.

Variation: As above, but using words that people hate.

Closure: Leader and group talk about what they have seen. How were words shown? How did people agree what to do? Did everyone agree on what makes a beautiful word? The leader talks with the group about how they feel.

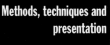

Part 3

Appendices

Chapter 7

Working with people with a learning disability

As always, we have a problem of terminology. We should no longer use the word 'handicap' but, as Chesner (1995) points out, to refer to 'learning difficulties' is misleading; she adopts, with reservations, the term 'learning disability'. Not only with language, but also with expectation of achievement, we have to deal with much misinformation, especially in groupwork. People with a learning disability are considered by some people as unable to be creative, artistic, responsive or receptive to groupwork. There are still assumptions that such people can only learn by rote and repetition, and that their affective levels of function are impaired.

We need to be clear that the full range of human emotion is present, even if pathways for its expression may be limited by internal or external forces. Furthermore, it is the author's own experience that these feelings can be explored through action methods and groupwork.

A newspaper reporter received a well-deserved metaphorical body blow when attending a drama group with people with a learning disability: shoving the microphone in front of various participants, he asked, "And which bit did you like?" One young man, with Down's syndrome, said, after looking round the room, "The girl with the dark hair."

However, things are changing. A recent episode of *A Touch of Frost* on UK television featured two actors with Down's in the storyline, and local residents and police alike displayed predictable prejudice and assumptions, even suspecting one of the two of child murder. The Frost character himself was lost for words when questioning the young woman: "And what do you both do when you are alone together?" "We make love and have sex," she said.

Groupwork guidelines for people with a learning disability are the same as for other types of group. Do not use material that is inappropriate or language that is inaccessible. Those seeking in-depth analysis and ways of working with learning disabilities should read Anna Chesner's *Dramatherapy for People with Learning Disabilities* and Ann Cattanach's *Drama for People with Special Needs* (1992).

Improvisation

Aim: Sharing, creativity

Time: 20 minutes

Materials and preparation: The group should be warmed up

Activity: For groups with limited skill at working together, the session can begin with the group leader telling a story, with the whole group putting actions to the story as it is being told. The leader could take the group on a journey, one that is already part of their lives, such as a visit to the local park. He would describe the journey there, how busy roads were crossed, transport used, what happened in the park, what refreshments people had and the journey home. Alternatively the leader could take them on a journey to places they had not been to, such as a desert, again describing the journey there, their means of travel and why they were in the desert. They could talk about the scenery, the people they met, how they refreshed themselves and the journey home.

Closure: The leader communicates with the group about the different ways of doing things. How does the group feel?

Sharing

Aim: Sharing activities

Time: 20 minutes

Materials and preparation: The group should be warmed up

Activity: The leader first asks the group to split up into pairs and tells them that they will be receiving instructions to do certain things with their partner. Then, depending on the skill of the players, he offers the following suggestions:

> Can you jump with your partner?
> Can you dance with your partner?
> Can you stay close to your partner while on the move?
> Can you be very small with your partner?
> Can you sit facing your partner and drive a car?
> Can you roll your partner up into a ball?
> Can you roll this 'ball' around the room?
> Can you swim through a sea of golden syrup with your partner?

Closure: The leader communicates with the group about how they feel.

Jungle

Aim:	Creating, leading, sharing
Time:	20 minutes
aterials and preparation:	The group should be warmed up
Activity:	The leader explains that the group are now invited to copy his actions and that, afterwards, anyone who wants to may, in turn, become the leader and lead the group through parts of the story.

The leader then mimes a trek into the jungle, clearing a path with a large bushknife, stopping to eat some fruit, taking leeches off his legs, imitating animals such as snakes, tigers, birds and monkeys. All the while, the rest of the group are in a line behind the leader, doing their best to copy the leader's movements. The leader should try to keep the line moving as rhythmically as possible. Still moving, the leader then says to the group, "I'm going to the back of the line. Now take turns, if you want to, imitating any animal in any way you want and the rest of the group will copy you." The leader goes to the back and, with the rest of the group, copies the actions of the person in front.

It does not matter if people cannot think of an animal: they just move any way they want and the rest of the group copies. If there is enough energy, they should try to keep this game going until the leader has worked back up through the line and is back at the front of the queue, thus giving everyone the opportunity to have a go.

Closure: The leader talks with the group about the different animals that were portrayed.

Musical hoops

Aim: Co-operation, creativity

Time: 10 minutes

Materials and preparation: A hula hoop for each person and a music system (or a drum or a leader prepared to sing)

Activity: Each person is given a hula hoop and invited to place it somewhere in the room so that it does not overlap onto someone else's. The leader explains that, when the music plays, everyone should dance or move around the room and when the music stops everyone should find a hoop and stand in it. That is round one. The game will continue in the same way, but after each round one hoop will be taken away and so people will have to share hoops. At the end, when there is only one hoop, everyone must try and share it, with at least some part of their body or wheelchair in the hoop. The leader then starts and stops the music.

Closure: The leader communicates with the group about how they feel. Did everyone manage to get into the last hoop?

Shouting hello

Aim: Making yourself heard

Time: 10–20 minutes

Materials and preparation: A helper if required

Activity: The leader stands at one end of the room with her back to the rest of the group. Everyone then shouts out as loud as they can, "Hello!" The leader then turns round to face the group and calls out the name of the first person she heard. This person steps forward two paces (some groups may need a helper to ensure that only the person whose name was called steps forward — they could be the 'Rule' police). The game carries on again, with everyone shouting "Hello" and the leader calling out the name of the person she heard, who takes two steps forward. This carries on until someone is close enough to touch the back of the leader.

The first person to touch the leader now takes the leader's place. Everyone else goes back to the other end of the room and the game starts again as before.

Closure: The leader talks with the group about how they feel.

Batman and Robin

Aim: Keeping a secret, co-operation, observation

Time: 10–20 minutes

Materials and preparation: An object such as a beanbag, a hat or a shoe

Activity: Everyone is invited to sit in a circle. An object, such as a hat, is chosen and everyone is given a chance to examine it. Two people are then chosen to be detectives Batman and Robin. These two people leave the room. While they are waiting outside the room the rest of the group choose a place to hide the hat. The two detectives are invited to come back and find the hat. The group can give whatever encouragement or misinformation they want. When the first pair have found the hat, the game continues with other pairs until everyone who wants to has had a go.

Closure: The leader talks with the group about how they feel.

Space walk

Aim: Experiencing space

Time: 10–15 minutes

Materials and preparation: None

Activity: The group leader should talk the group through the game, as follows: "Start exploring the space around the room. As you walk, 'feel' all the space around you, in front of you, behind you, around your feet, around your head, your armpits, the top of your head, inside your mouth. Feel the shape of your body as you walk around the room. As you walk, imagine that the space is actually touching you: your legs, face, feet and so on."

After a little while the leader can suggest other environments to experience, such as a swimming pool, the inside of a giant balloon or the inside of a long tube.

Closure: Talk about how the space felt. How do the group feel?

Hedgehog

Aim: Exploring relationships within the group, dealing with change

Time: 10 minutes (minimum)

Materials and preparation: The group should be thoroughly warmed up

Activity: The leader asks the group to get into pairs. One person in each pair pretends to be a hedgehog and curls up in a ball, so that they feel warm and safe. The other partner should now try and persuade them to uncurl and come and enjoy the world. The leader invites them to try many different verbal and non-verbal ways of enticing them. After a few minutes, each pair swaps over. After a few more minutes, the leader asks everyone to curl up as a hedgehog, feeling what it is like for a minute or so.

Closure: The leader talks with the group about the different ways of enticing someone to uncurl. What was it like to be all curled up? What got people to uncurl?

Presenting

Aim: Being positive about ourselves

Time: 20 minutes

Materials and preparation: None

Activity: The group are invited to form a circle. In turn, each person goes into the centre of the circle and introduces themselves, as if they were circus ringmasters, to the rest of the group, saying three positive things about themselves in the introduction. Everyone claps and that person then returns to the circle and another person goes to the centre and follows the same procedure. The game continues until everyone has had a go.

Closure: The leader talks with the group about how they feel.

How do they walk?

Aim: Movement, creativity

Time: 10–20 minutes

Materials and preparation: None

Activity: Group members line up, with their backs against one wall. The leader then calls out a type of person or an animal and members try to mimic how they feel that person or animal would walk by walking towards the opposite wall. In the course of this game the leader can call out a wide variety of names of animals, insects, fish, people or other 'beings' that the group try to mimic.

Closure: The leader talks with the group about how they feel.

Interviews

Aim: Being in the spotlight, exploring feelings

Time: 15–20 minutes

Materials and preparation: None

Activity: The leader and group together choose a topic that interests them, such as love, relationships, shopping, eating and so on. Now the leader divides the group into groups of three. Group members now prepare to interview each other on the chosen topic, taking it in turns to be interviewer, interviewee and audience. When everyone has had a go at each activity they are invited to form a circle.

Closure: The leader talks with the group about what came up in the different interviews. How do people feel?

Chapter 8

Optimum conditions

What is the ideal and can it be achieved? When thinking about this question, I am reminded of the times I have been in a supermarket looking for the *perfect* packet of biscuits. I walk up and down the supermarket aisle, scanning each shelf in turn, but the perfect packet never jumps out at me. I look at the same packets that I have seen before, hoping that this time one of them will be *just right*. The perfect packet never materializes and I end up choosing some biscuits that I *quite* like. I have spent up to 15 minutes in a kind of dream state on this little exercise and it amazes me that I still do it. There is no such thing as the perfect biscuit, just as there is no such thing as the perfect group or the perfect leader.

Anything short of perfection to a perfectionist is failure. It therefore follows that, if we are not chasing perfection, we are less likely to fail. If we want the ideal, we should not have to think *perfection*; rather we should think *suitability*. What is suitable for one group is not for another, but there are a few ideal conditions which, if they can be achieved, will help the smooth running of any group.

Space An appropriate space is important. A space is a space, so often we do not have any choice and we take what is given. If we do have a choice then the following points are worth thinking about.

Size The optimum size of the space depends upon the size of the group and what the group will be doing. If the group is sitting down in chairs, there only needs to be enough space for everyone to sit comfortably (in a circle?) and somewhere bags and coats can be left so that people do not trip over them. If the group are to do some kind of movement, play games or do exercises, a larger space is needed. A rule of thumb is that, if all the group members stand apart, they should be able to have at least a metre of space around them. Examples of suitable spaces are a hall, a classroom, a large front room, a playground (if it is sunny!), a warehouse and so on.

Windows All groups should be able to seal off the space from onlookers. This could mean covering up windows with black paper or with curtains. Remember that ventilation is important, particularly on a hot day, so an ability to open windows is also important.

Floor A wooden floor is nearly always the most appropriate to use. Wooden floors are warm and absorb shocks if people are exercising on them, or if someone falls over. A concrete floor should be avoided if at all possible.

Changing room If one is available, use it.

Electric points These are useful for tape recorders, kettles, projectors, special lighting and so on.

Time

We need to have time to participate in or to run groups. Members should know what the allotted time is and, if they are going to meet more than once, regular times should have been agreed. The following points should be borne in mind:

- How much time do you need?
- How much time do you have?
- If time is short, do not try to fit too much in: save it for next time or negotiate an extension. Remember that less and high-quality is better than more and mediocre.
- Keep timings consistent.
- Have the space booked for a secured amount of time.
- Do not let personal matters intrude upon group time.
- Make sure everyone knows the timings.

The group

We have talked much about 'the group' in this manual. Ideally the group members should be people that want to be there.

The group leader

Much has been said about the qualities of a good leader and different leaders need different qualities. The leader should be trained for the job in hand; have a good use of language; be honest; demonstrate genuine interest in people.

Equipment

All groups can make use of equipment at some time or other. Below are some examples.

Flip chart Flip charts can be good for presenting group ideas and information gathering (brainstorming). They can also be used for giving presentations. The large sheets are excellent for drawing pictures on.

Overhead projector Mainly used for giving presentations, overhead projectors are quite good for giving short bursts of information, bullet points for example, and they add atmosphere as they are usually used in a darkened room!

Slide projector If photographs need to be shown to a group, slides are the perfect tool.

Films There are many ways of showing films to a group. The video cassette recorder is probably favoured by most for its accessibility, ease of use and the range of films available. It is also easily used in conjunction with a video camera. A video is a far cheaper option than a 16 millimetre or 32 millimetre film. For groups with time and with limited budgets and who want to film the group in action for any particular reason, there is another option. Super 8 cameras and projectors can be obtained relatively easily at car boot sales or auctions and cost very little. The film is a little more difficult to pick up, but a good local camera shop could tell you where to find it (Kodak will process it).

Pens and paper These are very useful in many situations: drawing, writing notes, games, messages, instructions and so on.

A bag of goodies This is a bag full of objects such as soft toys, dolls, musical instruments, wooden blocks, crayons, note pads and balls. Such items are particularly useful if working with children or with certain therapy groups. A dramatherapist might call this a Pandora's box of ideas and creativity.

The leader's toolbox The group leader who is 'super efficient' and who has the resources will carry around the following items in a small sports bag for those unexpected difficulties: ten pens and pencils, an eraser, two different coloured marker pens, a phone card, an A4 and an A5 pad of paper, a ruler, a tape measure, a Swiss army knife, a roll of gaffer tape, a roll of Sellotape, a diary, a 13 amp and a 5 amp fuse, an electrical screwdriver, a torch, a packet of aspirin or paracetamol, a bag of boiled sweets or mints, a few tea bags and a few sachets of coffee, a small bottle of water and a good book.

Telephone

For group communication outside hours, booking members, promotional activities and so on, a telephone is a useful group asset.

Computer

This expensive addition is becoming more and more useful for individuals and for group use. A vast array of visual and interactive information is now available for computer users. Not only a useful typewriter, the computer can simulate reality. Computer owners have their own worldwide group, known as 'the Internet', where information can travel the world instantly from one computer to another.

Tape recorder

This is useful for recording group sessions, playing music in breaks or for doing warm-up, dance and movement routines.

Drum

A drum is very useful: a rhythm a day keeps the doctor away!

Resource packs

A pack with background information, follow-up material and so on can be useful for members in certain groups, such as a skills training workshop.

Finance

Groupwork can be done with no money, but this is not ideal. Money is usually needed for the following: salaries, space/room hire, equipment, transport, promotion and advertising, refreshments and all the resources and luxuries we want the group to have.

Chapter 9

A moment of enlightenment

Casework anecdotes

The following contributions were very kindly given by a wide range of people involved in many different types of group experience. They have been written in different styles, representing the heavier and lighter sides of group experience, and I hope they may be read to be enjoyed and as food for thought. I have made no changes apart from those necessary to maintain the anonymity of particular people or groups and the suppression of one or two explicit words. Otherwise the contributions speak for themselves.

It happened about eight years ago. I was involved with a group of medical students. They were senior students, finishing their second year of clinical studies, and most of them were going to be doctors in about a year or so. I cannot remember exactly what the purpose of our session was. I think it had something to do with preparing the students for a subsequent session when they would be playing 'doctor' to actors who would be playing 'patient'. In the course of the session we explored different sorts of 'doctor' and different sorts of 'patient' through role-play.

Bit by bit, something quite startling and entirely unexpected became apparent. The medical students were uninhibited and carefree in developing the character of the 'patient'. They had no problem in throwing themselves into their roles, and exploring the widest possible diversity of human behaviour. They enjoyed the notion that we are all different from each other, and they were happy to experiment with this in role-play. Boys played girls and girls played boys. They took on 'difficult parts', such as playing the elderly or characters quite unlike themselves. However, when it came to playing the role of 'doctor', all the medical students, even those who had been most imaginative in playing 'patient', were totally inhibited. They suddenly found that they were unable to develop any sort of range and that the role of 'doctor' was a straitjacket!

There were two surprises here. The first was the difference in the perception of 'patient' and 'doctor'. The second was that it should be the soon-to-be young doctors who were having trouble with the role of 'doctor'. Of course, the surprise was short lived. It soon became apparent that this was the very issue which needed to be addressed. The medical students had never considered the possibility that the role of 'doctor' could encompass as much variety as that of 'patient'. On the contrary, there was a presumption that 'doctor' was not a role at all.

Once this issue was brought out into the open, it led to a new perception. Instead of patients having to play a role to suit their doctor, why not the other way round? Why not doctors playing a role to suit their patients? This is the formula we have been developing ever since.

Robert Silman

Mayhem in Medellin

Medellin has a bad reputation. It is the drug centre of South America, if not the world, and the home of the infamous Medellin Cartel. A friend's house backs onto the house of the late Pablo Escobar. One hundred metres up the road is the house of the Ochoas. My friend has never known whether he lives in the safest or the most dangerous place in Colombia.

To the visitor from the outside, Medellin crackles with energy; its shopping centre is bursting with high-fashion boutiques. One can eat in Medellin as well as one can eat in Paris, at a fraction of the cost. Everywhere there is building. In Medellin, history has no significance. If you need something new, you simply pull down the old. Occasionally one is advised to avoid the next turning and to walk by some other road. One can hire killers easier and cheaper in Medellin than anywhere else. Medellin is the new Mahagonny. If you have money, it is the greatest place in which to be. If you are poor or unemployed, it is hell.

It is the easiest place in the world to run workshops. If you can't work in Medellin you should give up, retire, forget about theatre and therapy. The only problem lies in restraining them. The people of Medellin are always coming forward. In the streets, boys try to sell you cigarettes: "Buy some cigarettes." "I don't smoke." "It doesn't matter, buy some cigarettes." When you ask for four volunteers, there is a general stampede of people onto the floor. This is because you never get to say "four". As soon as you say, "Can I have ...", they are all out of their seats. You begin a game or exercise with, "The first rule is...", and they are already hard at it, oblivious of the second and third rules.

I have given several sets of workshops in Medellin. The first was in the Drama Department of the University of Antioquia. It wasn't really *in* so much as *with*. They turned out the whole staff and student bodies, more than 50 people. The workshop took place on the school stage, an enormous space. Medellin doesn't have a lot of theatre but is has three theatres with stages the size of football pitches, apart from the smaller ones, which is where the real theatre takes place. I was offered one of these vast spaces for a production of *The Beggar's Opera*, along with 94 actors and a full symphony orchestra.

It isn't easy working with 50 people in a huge space, especially when the anticipated drop-out never takes place and they all turn up for every session. But things went well, at the expense of my nerves, until I foolishly opted for a version of an exercise designed to illuminate master/ servant relationships in power hierarchies. This has always been non-controversial. Some underling is selected to perform some simple task, such as, say, preparing the room for a prestige function. A foreman is designated to instruct him in what is needed and to supervise his work. A second superior appears to check with the foreman how the work is going and a third superior appears to check with the second. A chain of command is set up until the boss arrives to make sure all is well. Originally the exercise begins as a clown exercise. Everyone above the worker is equipped with a rolled newspaper. The subordinates mock and pull faces at their superiors. If they are caught, the superior reinstates authority by hitting them with the newspaper. Beyond this stage, the group can work more subtly, drawing on their own experiences of the various strategies employed in hierarchies, whereby superiors maintain authority by denigrating subordinates and subordinates attempt to maintain or recover their self-respect by denigrating superiors. In any playing, either way, it soon becomes clear that the major stresses lie on the foreman and the managing director, one up from the bottom and one down from the top. It is a useful exercise in objectivizing and demystifying how bureaucratic institutions work, as well as a training ground for survival techniques.

In Medellin it provoked a pitched battle. No sooner had the clown version started when the game degenerated into a gleeful melee of people battering each other about the head with rolled-up newspapers, punctuated by howls of gleeful laughter. As the fun started, so more and more people joined in for the pleasure of hitting and being hit and the game sank in pleasurable violence.

There was little I could do to divert the course of all this. I couldn't raise my voice above the din to be heard, for a start. The fun had to run its course. When it had died down sufficiently to assert some control over the proceedings, I tried to hold an inquest into what had gone wrong. I discussed the original purpose of the exercise and wondered why it had taken the course it had. They listened with great interest as I outlined the nature of bureaucratic hierarchies. They found it fascinating as a picture of how things were in England and, to encourage me, they told me the game might work in Barraquilla on the coast, but, they assured me, things were not like that in Medellin. I learned a lesson. While we use games in training actors and in therapy on the principle that we are dealing with a universal feature of human life and interaction, which forms for us an international language that can leap over linguistic barriers, it is as well to remember that some games and exercises are determinedly culture-based and culture-bound. Nothing ventured, nothing gained. The failure led to a deeper understanding of the way things are in Medellin, but I have been very chary of using that unguarded approach elsewhere.   *Clive Barker*

Group consciousness

The one thing that has always stood out in my experience of groupwork is the universality of group consciousness and how it seems to reflect the unconscious process of the group leader.

An example of this is when I ran an introduction to dramatherapy for a mixed group who were seeking creative ways to express themselves once a week for ten weeks. From day one, the group was fragmented, so much so that throughout the ten weeks we were only together once as a whole group. Issues surrounding group members had begun to surface, in particular around one girl who had fast become the scapegoat for the rest of the group. Feelings of hostility and anger had been aroused, yet the girl concerned was always absent when the group were ready to address this. When she was present, those who had wished to raise the issue were not, and so it went on. Positive confrontation never took place. In the end the group spoke to empty chairs and did some role-play work to relieve the frustration temporarily.

In trying to understand what was happening and believing in the universality of group consciousness, I looked closely at my own situation. This was the last group I was to facilitate before moving house to a new area. A part of me had already moved and I was in pre-move chaos and nervous about the future. Although physically present, I felt I was just going through the motions and not really holding the group, providing the safety they needed. My supervisor astutely pointed out that perhaps I felt uneasy about my moving on and leaving the group somewhere that I didn't want to be myself. Through this insight into my own situation I was beginning to understand the level of insecurity present in the group.

I then suggested to the group that we devote a session to the subject of endings and new beginnings. It was through this that everyone began to reveal strong feelings of uncertainty about their own future and how held back they felt by their fears of what they were letting go and leaving behind. We then presented these feelings in an improvisation where, quite naturally and wonderfully, all the issues surrounding the scapegoat were positively addressed and resolved through the roles they played. This whole experience showed me the importance of recognizing my own process in my role as group facilitator, and that I play an active part in helping a group to progress.

Another example of linked consciousness was with an already established group who had been meeting regularly for five weeks. Up to this point, the sessions had included various trust games, improvisations on thematic ideas derived from the group and some sculpting work. I did not feel the group were wanting to work to a great depth; in fact they visibly backed off from any confrontational work, so I kept on with trust building and endeavoured to keep their creative imagination stimulated in the hope that they would remain interested and open to new experiences.

Then someone pointed out that they wanted more and expressed some dissatisfaction in my not providing appropriate material for them to work with. This got me to thinking, "If they want more, why don't they take more? Just who is responsible for the well-being of this group?" Although I had clearly stated at the start, "The success of this group is up to you. You will get out what you put in", I came to the conclusion that it was probably part of my role as facilitator to act as a mirror to the group in order to assist them in the process of enactment and change.

In my follow-up report, it was interesting to notice that my mind had begun to question whether, in my wanting the group to have ample stimulation, they got what was appropriate for the moment. In providing a varied and entertaining forum for creative exploration I had probably denied them the opportunity for working with their resistance to confrontation. It seems I had visibly backed off subsequently, reflecting the feelings of the group.

I am still left wondering whether it was the chicken or the egg.

Rachael Perry

The unstructured group

Some years ago I attended a week's course on group dynamics run by a well-known national organization. For the first day and a half, the 50 people there were split into groups of about eight from similar backgrounds; for the next day and a half we were in groups from disparate backgrounds; then we gathered in one large group and experimented with different seating plans, and finally we broke into free-formed groups which interacted with each other. All the usual lessons were learned by self-discovery, with the tutors acting almost entirely passively and only contributing when an important point had been missed. I recall one incident which was certainly not planned.

Our group of eight from disparate backgrounds had gathered for its second session shortly after breakfast on day three. It was immediately apparent that Harry was absent. The tutor came in and sat down in his customary silent manner. We talked in a desultory way about the lessons we had learnt the previous day but the discussion had a sense of being simply to fill the time while we waited for Harry to appear. Occasionally someone would look at their watch and wonder out loud why he was so late. Someone recalled that he had been at the bar late the previous night. Someone else mentioned that he had looked tired and under stress. Another person who was using the room next to him said that he hadn't heard him getting up that morning. I suggested that perhaps he had dropped out and gone home as one or two other people had done. Finally the tutor interrupted to point out that the absence of Harry had dominated our thoughts for over an hour. "Why," he asked, "if you feel so concerned about him, doesn't someone go and check his room to see if he is still alive?" There was a stampede from the room and ten minutes later an unshaven and rather sheepish Harry joined us. He had simply overslept! We were appropriately angry at his lack of self-discipline and told him how much time he had wasted. Or had we wasted it? It was apparent on mature reflection that a member who is absent from a small group can be as potent as anyone actually there – indeed even more so – and we had learnt a valuable lesson. The secondary lesson was that, in this somewhat unusually unstructured group where no-one had authority or responsibility, it needed the stimulus of an external authority (the tutor) to trigger the necessary action.

Bill Davis

Leaders can split the group and can bond the group

I'm a performing artist and have worked with many different groups, personalities, cultures and lifestyles. These differences often dictate the format for a group's dynamics. I have found that groups work best when each individual member's aims and objectives are the same. I feel that the smaller the group the better it works.

In my teens, with a few friends, we started a 'school band'. We were disliked by our music teacher – probably because we used the school's facilities along with the facilities of a neighbouring school. Also no-one in the band had chosen music as an option. This I feel helped with our bonding: five years after school we were still going strong, were better musically and we remained focused. Our friendships seemed solid and that alone is what held the band together. Somehow (don't ask me how) we got a manager and, for reasons unknown to me still to this day, the manager managed to split up this group friendship and fragment our focus. I believe that our youth and ignorance allowed this to happen.

Just as one person can smash up a group's dynamics, it can also take one person to create a focus and bonding. A few years ago I performed in a musical extravaganza that toured all over the country. Still to this day it has to be the greatest group feeling I have had: 12 actors, dancers and musicians mostly unknown to each other; an epic play never before performed; and a director with a belief and dream to see his creation come alive. The 'groupwork' was the central part of the rehearsal process; the script was almost secondary. The building of the group was the success of the play. If one person in the play was kicked in the leg then we all limped. I can't work out how he made so many people from so many different lifestyles entwine so well, but he did. We all lived and slept the play 100 per cent. Day and night everything was solid and focused. A leader with charisma and a vision brought us together and took us on a journey of success.

Glenn Dallas

An anecdote

I was working with a group of first year students at the beginning of their second semester. They had just completed a four-week group-devised performance project and there were plenty of unresolved and unanalysed conflicts in the group. Part of the problem with the group's final presentation, as I saw it, was that they'd failed to keep the multiplicity of narratives in the group by not recognizing difference as a source of creative energy.

In this semester we were going to be working with questions of leadership, responsibility, oppression, community and co-operation. In this first session I decided to make difficulties for my role as leader/facilitator – something which I've done with varying degrees of success on many other occasions with different groups. I did this initially through an exercise which I won't describe here; I think it's important just to reveal some of the context for what follows. I also set up games which involved people in leader/follower and facilitator/facilitated roles. For what follows, the most important of these was a musical version of 'follow-the-leader' where leadership was transferred around the group through the passing and wearing of a hat.

When we were discussing the various questions that arose from people's experiences of the exercises, one member of the group wondered how the 'follow-the-leader' exercise would work without music. I gave him the hat. Five members (all women) of the 16-strong group refused to join in by remaining silently seated on the floor. The rest of the group (and I joined in – following the leader) tried to encourage the others to join in with words, songs and gestures, and used physical force at one point to persuade/coerce the minority to join their 'community'. One moment of powerful conflict was when the leading group sang 'Up! Up! Up!' and the dissenters sang 'Down! Down! Down!', the minority culture asserting itself in direct opposition to the majority group which was setting the agenda to a large extent. When physical force was used, two members of the minority group held on to each other and held their ground and two of the three who had been forcibly removed returned.

When the game ended, we shared our experiences. Most people in the majority group felt that the minority were 'spoiling things' by not joining in and used the exercise as an example of some of the difficulties which the group had experienced during their devising process. It was important to clarify at this moment whether or not those people who had refused to follow the leader were perceived by the others as always frustrating group effort: they weren't. The person who was coerced into the main body and remained was in a very good position to share the feelings of both groups. When she was in the small group she shared the feeling that the others had no right to dictate to her, but when she joined the large group she shared their point of view and found her former colleagues' behaviour to be frustrating.

Because the majority group were following the person with the hat, and this leader was sanctioned by the rules of the game and by the tutor (who joined in), they felt that they had a legitimate grievance against the minority who were, in their eyes, threatening the integrity of the group.

The minority group, on the other hand, could and did appeal to another set of rules to justify their action: that the session was about leadership, that they were encouraged to question, that the tutor himself had explored a form of refusal at the beginning of the session. That the tutor did nothing to enforce their co-operation was seen also as an implicit authorization for what they were doing. (In both cases, clearly, the tutor's authority is used to justify two strongly opposing ways of behaving, but this question was left unexplored.)

The feedback from this exercise led to further exploration of grievances within the group which had arisen as a result of the devising work. I went away excited by the wealth of material that had been generated by a simple, unplanned, exercise in which so many questions of power, control, oppression, resistance, hegemony, dominance, community and ethics were raised.

Franc Chamberlain

Community theatre

I was working with a student group exploring forms of community theatre. It was several weeks into the term. The preceding sessions had been generally enjoyable but there had been various minor confrontations. The group appeared to get on well but were not cohesive, and they were going to have to start working together to devise a performance to be presented at the end of term; this knowledge gave me – and probably some of the group – a certain unease.

In this particular session we were to work practically on some of Boal's techniques, beginning with Image Theatre. I had a plan for the morning but the first problem was that several of the group were absent; this interfered significantly with a number of exercises I'd intended to do. I decided while we were doing a warm-up that I'd shift the focus for the session and use Boal's techniques to look directly at the group itself as a 'community' (or not, as the case may be).

Having introduced the basic techniques, I invited a volunteer to 'sculpt' an image using the group to *represent* the group, as she saw it. The student in question quickly drew us into a circle (me included) facing each other, holding hands, each of us smiling. I recognized the 'face' that she was illustrating; on one level, the group got on very well and were friendly, with plenty of laughs, and had quite a comfortable relationship with me, as their course leader. I waited to see if the image would be challenged, however, which it was almost immediately: "I don't see us like that at all!"

The second volunteer took several minutes to sculpt his image. He began by placing me standing on a chair, then draped someone's cardigan over my head so I was blind. I was aware of people being moved into places behind and in front of me, but I could only see later what kind of image had been constructed. The whole sculpture was highly complex. The overall impression involved elements of struggle, pulling different ways, physical support, affection, aggression. I was not the only member who had been 'stifled'; another person – a particularly quiet member of the group – had her head inside a jumper someone else was *wearing* … I appeared to be quite physically isolated but, behind my chair, someone was supporting me – or possibly trying to pull me off; as it happened, this person was one of the most forceful contributors and was possibly the student most knowledgeable about the issues raised by the course.

Most of the group had plenty to say about the image they had been sculpted into. Some found it too 'surreal' to be understandable, typical (they felt) of that particular student's approach. Others resented the implied conflicts within the group that were clearly indicated in the image.

This may have been to do with fear; a group project lay ahead, and it might be felt preferable to preserve at least the illusion of being a 'good group' rather than to bring up more than there was time to deal with. To still others, it was clearly a relief that someone had found a way to reveal some of the problems that had been under the group's surface. A question arose: were we representing *ourselves*, or simply being 'bodies'? In my position on the chair, I was clearly cast as 'teacher'; we considered this, and recognized that, however comfortable our relationship might seem, the difference between us remained: they were the ones being assessed. The quiet student whose head had been covered felt embarrassed, I think, at having attention drawn to her; she acknowledged herself as shy and somewhat reluctant to contribute, but insisted that she was responsible for this and rarely felt stifled by other members. The student supporting/pulling me had been placed there, the sculptor said, "because I see him as the most obvious leader within the group, and in a way as a challenge to your [that is, the tutor's] authority". This calm statement produced a minor sensation: shock from some that 'group dynamics' were being exposed in this way, embarrassed denial from the student in question, forceful assertions from others that he was *not* the leader, supportive reactions towards me (perhaps thinking I might feel the group lacked faith in me as a leader).

It was mainly the above 'interpretations' that led some members to request that, if we continued with the exercise, we use people *non-specifically* to avoid being too personal. This was immediately contested: wasn't the whole point to be personal, to face up to how we were operating in the group, how others perceived us, and so on? Another argument was offered: if we used people *as themselves*, how could we represent another, highly significant, faction, the absentees?

In the course of the session we worked both ways, using people as themselves and also more generally, as 'bodies'. The group requested that I make an image – "Show us how *you* see us" – which I did; it was a relief to have a creative way to express my frustrations about aspects of the group's behaviour, but it also taught me that some of my 'irritations' were out of all proportion to the crime. As the work progressed we moved on to create 'ideal' images of how we'd like the group to be, and to look then at 'transitional' images: how could the group take steps to improve?

The session was clearly very valuable, and the images stuck in the group's minds for a long time afterwards. A huge amount had come up – personal and impersonal, for the students and for myself. The only real problem was that not all the group had been there to explore the issues. In a way, though, it was the problem of absenteeism that had led me to initiate the work in the first place. It would be a mistake to think that this sort of exercise is only appropriate when there's trouble, however; if we had used these or similar techniques earlier on, some of the later difficulties might possibly have been avoided.

Frances Babbage

The picture game

One of the ways in which I was involved in groupwork, when I was a counsellor, was to co-lead groups for 'self-awareness and confidence building'. These were closed groups of eight sessions with about 12 members, one evening a week. The groups consisted of members of the public and ex-Relate clients. As well as doing a training in 'understanding groups and group leadership', I felt that it was important to experience being in one of the groups as a client before I started co-leading.

I found one of the most effective exercises, aimed at identifying emotions and not making assumptions, was 'The Picture Game', which we played in the second session. When we came into our room that evening, we noticed that there were many different pictures, taken mainly from magazines and newspapers, put up on the walls. We had to walk round the room in silence and jot down the first emotion we felt as we looked at the numbered pictures.

Back in our group circle, we read out the emotion which each image had triggered and one of the leaders collated them on a flip chart. Two points quickly emerged. First, one member of the group denied feeling anything at all, although we had already done work on acknowledging that we are always feeling something. His behaviour, of not being prepared to share anything, was not confronted by the group at this stage. Discussing this in a later session, it emerged that the group members were reluctant to be confrontational so soon; preserving the group cohesion was more important than questioning one member.

The second point was that there was a complete mixture of responses given for each picture; not one of them evoked a unanimous emotion. For example, a large bonfire burning on the edge of a field produced feelings ranging from excitement (thinking of the Fifth of November), to fear (a burning house), delight, pain (an accident), cosiness (winter evenings) and pleasure (memories of a grandfather).

A picture of a bullfight evoked emotions of happiness (a lovely day on holiday), humour (a matador being chased), disgust, fear and sadness. An old woman peering round a net curtain brought up feelings as varied as happiness (grandchildren arriving) and dread (loneliness of old age). A new-born baby in a hospital theatre being held by a surgeon mostly caused expressions of pleasure, joy, relief or excitement. For one member of the group, who was a nurse, it produced anxiety because she knew that a doctor would not be present for a normal delivery.

This game was a powerful way of bringing home to the group the dangers of making assumptions about other people's feelings. It highlighted the fact that we all interpret what we see through our own individual past experiences and needs. It was a useful reminder, for the sessions which followed, of the importance of checking the feelings of other members. It also proved valuable for relationships outside the group.

Frances Davis

Strangers

In a group seminar with 130 participants we were asked to form ourselves into smaller groups of around six people, to elect a leader and to exchange telephone numbers so we could support each other in our work during the rest of the seminar series. Six of us in the row I was seated in gathered together, chose a leader and began exchanging numbers.

Two minutes later the seminar leader approached our group and asked us if we would mind adding another person, who had had to leave early, to the group. There was a noticeable pause before we responded to the request, during which we all fought with the same instant reaction – we had bonded so quickly that none of us wanted to allow a stranger into the group. Two minutes before we had all been strangers to each other!

Myfanwy Harrington

Overseas walking groups

I have been a tour leader for five years for a firm who run overseas walking holidays in the mountains. Groups of people from many different backgrounds – teachers to engine drivers – spend two weeks based at a hotel in a foreign country. Each day they walk for six to seven hours and then spend their evenings together. The question of why some groups become close and cohesive (why they gel) and why others remain as two dozen individuals has always been a source of fascination to me, particularly as the groups which gel are a pleasure to lead and the others are such hard work. It doesn't seem to depend on the leader – my character remains relatively unchanged through a succession of groups – it seems to need one of a number of factors to occur. Cohesive groups often have one or two strong personalities, people who organize evenings activities or have a good sense of humour. Another binding factor is a shared example of a sing-song after supper. A third factor which creates

cohesion is the presence of someone in a group who becomes the focus of attention. The group clown is an example, as the following anecdote reveals.

Gordon was noticeable as soon as he got off the aircraft. Rather overweight, wearing glasses and in his early 30s, he seemed somewhat unco-ordinated and not my idea of a natural mountain walker. In conversation in the bus, it transpired that he was a bachelor and held a junior post in local government. From the cameras he was festooned with it was apparent that he was mad about photography. It was his first walking holiday, indeed his first holiday abroad, urged on him by his mother who felt 'he ought to go out and meet a few people'. Next morning he proudly appeared for the first walk with a selection of cameras around his neck and wearing his new boots. Already he was eliciting a few sniggers from the more experienced walkers. Within ten minutes he was 100 yards behind the rest of the group, and after another ten minutes he had blisters. He had bought the sort of boots suitable for the north face of the Eiger, but totally inappropriate for a brisk walk around the foothills of the Alps. He had to return to the hotel and change into gym shoes, which he wore for the rest of the holiday. His comical expression at his own misfortune immediately got him elected as the group clown – a role he seemed quite familiar with.

Thereafter he played the role for all it was worth and the group warmed to his performance. "When are we going to stop for lunch?" he would ask, about half an hour after starting the walk, to guffaws from the group. He would drop things, fall over rocks, forget to bring his picnic or, if he remembered to bring it, it would include totally unsuitable French delicacies which spread themselves all over the insides of his rucksack – more merriment from the group, who felt a cosy sense of superiority over this walking disaster. After three days, he fell madly in love with a pretty waitress at a local cafe in the village. He couldn't speak a word of French and she couldn't speak a word of English. His passion was unreciprocated, to such a degree that it was not until the last day of the holiday that she realized his eagerness to take so many photos of the cafe had anything to do with her. Observing other people's infatuations is often comical, but for the group it was just part of the clown's role.

The holiday ended and the group went home. I judged the group a close one – it had a strong identity, but at what cost? Were they exploiting Gordon? How far removed was Gordon from the village simpleton who in days gone by provided a similar focus in rural communities? Gordon seemed aware of his role and didn't seem unhappy with it. Not being very successful in his professional life or, apparently, in his personal relationships with women, it seemed to give him almost a perverse pleasure to be the focus of attention, whatever its cause. Popularity of a sort, but was it hurting underneath? I made a conscious effort to talk to him outside the role he had adopted and found him a sensitive person; we remained in correspondence for quite long afterwards. However, thinking about it later, I felt embarrassed that I had not made more effort to prevent his exploitation, which provided such an easy path to group cohesion.

Bill Davis

The large mansion

This was my first experience in true adult teaching. Groups of between 15 and 20 adult returners aged from 23 to 60 were attending a 21-week intensive humanities course which could offer, amongst other things, the chance of access to higher education. Members 'lived in' – the college was a large mansion set in its own estate.

One particular aspect of this course is that it attracted many people who felt that they were at a crossroads in their life because of some event or calamity which had given them cause to reappraise their ambitions. Often they were seeking a solution or direction, and were hoping the course would provide the answer. This created some extreme stresses within these groups which led to heated arguments in class and many fractious interactions outside the lecture room. There were also those who formed relationships within the close confines of a residential college, which in turn created other tensions in the group. Here are a few of the challenges that arose.

1 An ex-soldier who had served in Northern Ireland took exception to a comment from a left-wing group member who expressed a view that the British Army in Northern Ireland were merely mercenaries acting on behalf of a repressive regime to quell people's desire for self-determination. It took rapid intervention from the lecturer and a willingness on the part of the socialist to rephrase his point of view to defuse a potentially explosive situation which almost became a fist fight.

2 A provocative female member of the group, after making eyes at several of the male students, formed a relationship with one of them which drove a wedge between two halves of the group and almost caused it to disintegrate. The problem was exacerbated by certain disinformation from each of the two people involved, which led other group members to perceive that one or the other of the couple involved was being harassed by the other partner.

3 Individuals who not only had great difficulty coming to terms with the workload demanded of them but also found difficulty in taking advantage

of help and support that was offered, dipped out from some classes because of the effects of drugs and/or alcohol, and were eventually asked to leave.

4 A middle-aged female student was persuaded to attend a class dressed as a schoolgirl (in the St Trinian's mode), complete with pigtails and an apple for the teacher. This incident happened twice, with two different ladies, on two unconnected consecutive courses, and gave me a lot of heart-searching about unintentional messages that I might be transmitting. My response on both occasions was the same, to accept the situation in good humour and carry on as though nothing particularly unusual had happened.

The classroom experience of such groups was characterized by several features relating to different personality types:

1 The vocal and dogmatic student who had arrived with a particular set of values and wanted everyone else to accept that these were the only true and correct ones to have.

2 The intelligent but underconfident students who went through agonies of self-doubt before recognizing their own worth. They often had difficulty in participating in class and their contributions were overwhelmed by more vocal students unless the lecturer took positive steps to allow them space.

3 The less academic but overconfident student who challenged all low grades and tried to bully lecturers into admitting that the grades awarded should be improved. Not to be confused with genuine situations where the grade was, quite rightly, improved on appeal.

4 The student who lacked academic ability but whose persistence led to the resubmission of the same assignment up to four times in rapid succession in an attempt to improve their grade after feedback from the tutor.

5 The alcoholic student who was often late for the first class of the day after late-night drinking sessions.

The management of such groups presents a particular challenge. The tutor has to maintain a fine balance between encouragement and honest criticism, so that the underconfident are not destroyed while the overconfident come to recognize areas where they could improve. Another challenge is maintaining a professional distance from students while remaining empathetic to their needs.

One thing is clear. The open-minded and reflective tutor can learn much about group behaviour when teaching in adult education, but, while general forecasts of likely group responses to particular inputs can be made, no precise outcome can ever be guaranteed. It remains the key to the lecturer's art that one must always be alert for signals from the group about their appreciation and understanding (or lack of it) of the topic under discussion, and be prepared either to go back over the explanation or even change the method of delivery in order to achieve a successful outcome for the group.

David Dean

Highs and lows of group experience

Attempting to work in a humanistically, therapeutically oriented way in an educational setting is a challenge in itself. Add to that the main theme subjects of death, dying and bereavement, sexuality and Aids, and the recipe is potentially explosive. Sometimes the fuse ignites, and the explosion may be emotional and creative rather than destructive. At other times, the dynamics of the group may be orchestrated by individuals who bring their own agenda, and group members may unwittingly follow a leader who is working out their own frustration, anger or pain, perhaps quite legitimately, but at the expense of group cohesion and a more integrated experience.

That is not to say that such an intervention is unhelpful. It may be a force for change in ways that are not at first evident. Some of the finest coursework ever seen on a two-week Aids care programme came from students who had unknowingly accompanied a student on a personal loss journey. The challenges offered by this student ranged from criticism of the course structure and facilitators to verbal abuse directed at other course members. Although this took place in the context of a drama enactment, very real and strong emotions were stirred, and the time spent in processing and reflection was crucial. So often, this is neglected in educational settings where 'role-play' is used. Tutors attend a short course in the subject and enthusiastically hurl themselves into scenarios at every possible opportunity. Complicated scenes are set and elaborate character plots devised. The initial warm-up to put the group into the mood may be overlooked and, at the end of the piece, the 'de-roling' consists of name or word games such as 'My name is Jean and I like jelly'. This is supposed to restore emotional balance and the group moves to something else.

In the HIV/Aids field, it has become the practice to explore issues of personal sexuality as a way of understanding difference in others. For me, an unforgettable experience in a group occurred when the nurse tutor

asked us to describe our first sexual experience to the person sitting next to us! I am no prude, but this pressed my personal buttons, personally and professionally. When I challenged the group leader, I was assured that he had done it this way many times before, and everyone loved talking about sex! What about the adult whose first sexual experience was as a child, in an abusive situation? No thought had been given to the consequences of asking such a question in a public setting. Aware as I am that this was not a personal therapy group, I do not think that such risks are justified in the name of education. Another instance, in which 'humour' was associated with sexual activity, also caused some personal discomfort.

Students had been asked to devise a suitable ending for a course, in which many issues of life and death had been explored. The thinking was to use ritual as a way of facilitating closure to the life of the group, and to separate from each other in a meaningful way. Group members chose to use a version of pass the parcel, in which forfeits were involved. The group manipulated the situation so that I found myself having to put a condom on a very large courgette … with my mouth. Faced with the choice of opting out and appearing a spoilsport, or undertaking the task and feeling humiliated, I chose the latter. I very much regret that I compromised my integrity in this way, as I am sure the majority of the group were supportive of me, rather than the person who set this up. Again, personal agendas had manipulated the group for purposes which were not entirely honest. The experience was, however, meaningful.

As course director, my most positive experiences in groups over many years have involved the use of action methods to re-create difficult life experiences. Using an approach drawn from Psychodrama, I have facilitated workshops in which group members prepare to face their own death, or support others on their journeys. This work involves a certain degree of risk, but the climate is carefully set, and the pace is never hurried. Resistance to 'role-play' is overcome by ensuring that group members only take part voluntarily and accept the risk that is involved. In suggesting that there is a risk, I do not mean danger to life, of course, but that very carefully buried or concealed aspects of a person's life may come to the surface. In facilitating potential catharsis, I am not seeking a life-changing experience or transformation. I am providing an opportunity fully to face up to life as it is now, reflecting on the journey that has been travelled, with the opportunity to think about the future. The existential reality of the nature of the loss or changed circumstances is fully brought home to the protagonist and to the audience who in their 'spect-actor' (a mixture of spectator and actor) role feel very strong emotions as the story unfolds. Elaborate plots are not necessary, as we are working with the material of life itself. Students on a life and death studies course have accompanied their peers on journeys to prepare for the death of a close relative, most recently a mother, and then, when this event happened in reality, have been able to support them in their grief.

To exclude students from groups on the grounds that their loss experience has been too recent, as many counselling organizations seem to do, is to deny the opportunity for a rich and beautiful experience, which mirrors the approach that we are attempting to prepare for in our professional roles. Using the arts, encouraging students to draw on many creative forms of expression in their coursework, has many benefits, and the sequence of drama, reflection and creative recording through literature, music and image make education a truly therapeutic possibility.

Cyril Ives

The dramatherapy group as an agency for change of stereotyped behaviour

The scene is set in a dramatherapy group for inpatients in a hospital for people with long-term mental health problems. There were six people in the group – four women and two men – and two helpers as well as the group leader. Many of the people had difficulty in staying in the here and now, and also displayed rigidity in decision making and living. Movement was repetitive and statements were repeated again and again. The dramatherapy was being used to see if patterns could be interrupted and whether movement could change into new shapes, and sound and speech patterns could vary.

One member of the group spent a lot of time rocking in a corner and moaning to himself. Every attempt to bring him into the group was greeted by angry gestures and turning away, and a resumption of the rocking. Perhaps we needed to rethink this through? How could we integrate this man into the group? I asked the helpers afterwards, when we met to discuss and record what we had done. Someone said, "Perhaps we could try integrating the group into the man instead of the man into the group." We sat in stunned silence. What an amazing idea. But how? We all brainstormed possible ideas that we could try in the next session and came up with the following plan, based on our regular 'mirroring work', where people follow another's movements or sounds as accurately as they can.

One helper was to sit as near the person as he would allow and gently mirror the rocking and the moaning. Meanwhile the remainder of the group established a group movement: each individual was asked to contribute their own movement; the group repeated each individual's movement, and this way built up a set of movement patterns. When it came to the turn of the person rocking, the helper did his movement and everyone repeated it. The effect was startling. He immediately turned round and repeated his movement and everyone again copied him. Slowly, over the weeks, he was able to join the group in simple movements and sounds. It seemed this initial idea of the group going to him rather than him having to come to the group was the trigger for a change in behaviour.

Sue Emmy Jennings

Experience of groupwork

About ten years ago, I joined an evening class in Battersea called 'An Introduction to Counselling and Group Work'. It was the early boom of the rush to get on the counselling bandwagon. Everybody was a counsellor, or knew somebody who was, or wanted to be one, or spent time arguing that it wasn't them who needed the counselling, it was that irritating sod over there. I fitted into most of the categories.

There were about ten of us in the group. It should have been fun. Party games about getting to know you. A network of support. It was nothing of the kind. It wasn't that this was some kamikaze class: the tutor was gentle and considerate. She took everyday situations about relationships that we had experienced. For one session she asked each of us, using class members, to put our personal histories to rights. Family sculpting, I think it was called. Members placed a 'Dad' There (where he had never been), put a 'Husband' Right Here, (turned to face his wife), escorted 'Brother' Out Of The Door (this time he'll have to stay out) and so on. I won't tell you what I sculpted – we don't have to reveal outside the security of the group, you know, and my sculpting surprised even me. The gist of it for me was live and let live.

It was the coins exercise that threw me. It should have been a doddle. Which is where you learn that you should never assume that you, or anybody else, relate to the world in the same way. Take five pennies. Take a circle of ten people. Ask each in turn to give the coins to one or more members of the circle. Say ready, steady, go, and watch the results. Being first, I handed a coin each to the first five in the circle. The next person, of course, would carry on from where I had left off, ensuring an even distribution.

Of course it didn't work out that way. Two unrelated members of the circle were unable to do the exercise. Not just unable, but were reduced to tears, tremors, shock. One stood in the middle of the circle, paralysed. The other wouldn't even rise from the chair. Task abandoned for autopsy. It would be difficult for me to explain what happened, seeing that this is obviously a personal blind spot. What could be simpler? My own state of shock at the abandoned task arose from seeing such naked vulnerability attached, not to the stock checklist of likely trauma-inducing abuses or accidents, but to five pennies. The broken two spoke brokenly of jealousies, birthdays, Christmas, favouritism, hurt, anger. Which explains nothing about the way the exercise itself became a monster. The groupwork didn't provide answers there.

I've been treading on glass since, having been unsettled by this demonstration of the inability to detach, this burden of carting seemingly minor childhood resentments around like giant suitcases. But it's very wearing trying to be extra-sensitive. Usually I just take the risk, knowing that I'm offending somebody's sensibilities most of the time. It's impossible to anticipate such psychological landmines in others. One's own are no basis for making assumptions.   *Chloe Gerhardt*

My pregnant belly

the ... motionless moment when our future steps into us.

(Rainer Maria Rilke)

My oldest friend is an artist who has recently found herself struggling with her creative process. The process has become one of great personal risk taking. Life experience she once viewed as unspeakable is now exposed in her work. She is the friend with whom I have shared some of my greatest coming-of-age experiences.

I am nine months pregnant with my first child. She is the mother of two. Recently we spent an afternoon casting my pregnant belly in plaster of Paris gauze for a piece she is creating that will explore the 'landscape of motherhood'. Shortly after this intimate happening, I had a dream.

I am sitting with my friend, the artist, in her studio and we are discussing the challenge that she is facing in her art. The studio has windows that are open wide onto a tropical, densely vegetated landscape.

I am overcome with emotion, I want to help her, to 'free' her from her struggle. I want to reassure her that she is, indeed, on an important path. I see her risking. I want to risk, too.

As I move towards her, I suddenly find myself in a narrow clear plastic tube. This tube resembles a box that in my waking life I have been storing baby clothes in. The tube barely fits around my head. There is no air in the tube and I am suffocating.

I am no longer aware of my friend's entire body. She now hangs like a precious icon at the end of this long tube at a great distance from me. Without the ability to breathe, I find myself unable to 'get to her'. I am feeling frightened. I feel a failure. I wake from my dream.

In my last dramatherapy group before giving birth I share this dream. Aside from some initial associations (for example, the tube is a birth canal, my impending rebirth into a new role of motherhood, my fear of failure in this role), I feel unclear about this dream. What is more, there is a part of me that is afraid to uncover any holistic understanding. Perceiving this dream through its elements feels less threatening.

I am invited to enact my dream with the group. I identify three roles for the enactment: the two women and the plastic tube/birth canal. In the enactment I cast the other two female members of our group as 'The Artist' and 'Maria'. The woman whom I choose to play 'The Artist' has been a powerful presence for me in the group. I was initially put off by and envious of her ability to take so much space in the group. I have grown to feel a strong bond with her. I long to emulate the healthy emotional abandon she demonstrates in the group, in my own life.

'Maria' is the person whom I view as the most cerebral member of our group. She is thoughtful and introspective. She is less a woman of action than a woman of presence. In that capacity she is often caring for others but is rarely cared for by others. I, too, have difficulty letting others care for me.

Robert, the therapist, offers to play 'The Plastic/Tube Birth Canal'. It is not usual that he engages directly in an enactment. I am intrigued that lately he has begun to 'play' more with us. The other male member of our group, suffering from a back ailment, will double for 'The Birth Canal' and play additional roles in the enactment.

I sculpt the scene. I place 'The Artist', seated, straddling a wooden box, with her hands cupping her face in despair. I give her no words. I ask the woman playing 'Maria' to lie lengthwise on the ground, perpendicular to 'The Artist'. 'Maria' is advised to move with a weightedness and weakness throughout her body. I loosely tie a scarf around her nose and mouth to simulate a sensation of lack of oxygen. 'Maria' is also told to make every effort to get to 'The Artist'. I then instruct Robert in the role of 'The Birth Canal' to find a place near 'Maria' where he can physically offer resistance to her effort to move forward.

The enactment begins. 'The Artist', without my instruction to do so, immediately becomes verbal. She encourages and supports 'Maria' in her effort to get to her. The true role becomes instantaneously clear to me. 'The Artist' is the birth mother. Overcoming her despair that the hoped-for event may not result, 'The Artist' speaks with a singleness of purpose and great anticipation. She encourages her 'creation' not to give up hope. She is unrelenting, like a force of nature; she is unbound, like a divine entity. She is self and selfless. She is 'Mother'.

'The Birth Canal' also speaks. As 'The Birth Canal' speaks, its role in this enactment also becomes clear. 'The Birth Canal' is the voice, the presence, of repression. 'Maria', meanwhile, is struggling for breath. She is floundering, unable to find direction. In a small voice, barely audible, she all but accepts her failure to achieve her goal.

As the interaction between the three takes on a heightened tone, 'The Birth Canal' suddenly and mysteriously gives way. I am surprised. This did not happen in my dream. This is the release that I had hoped for and yet I am frightened by this development and of what may happen next. 'The Artist' does not hesitate. She sweeps her creation into her arms like a magnificent treasure. 'The Birth Canal' silently rolls out of tableau. The scene is now an interaction between the creator and her creation. 'Maria' is fatigued. She lies against 'The Artist's' breast. She is stroked, soothed, and welcomed into this new relationship.

I understand, at this moment, that this enactment has been a birth. I want to become part of 'The Artist', to share in the silent rapture. I ask myself, "Am I able to do such a remarkable thing as give birth?" The group has become the birth mother.

After a while, as we look after 'Maria', I find myself gaining distance on the event. I begin to see how this event has enhanced my impressions of the other group members. I see that the woman playing 'The Artist', herself the product of poor mothering, has an incredible *gift* for mothering. I see the woman playing 'Maria' allow herself to be cared for. I see the male group member who is often afraid to make physical and emotional contact, participate fully, silently, and without lengthy justification, as 'The Birth Mother'.

I also have an enhanced experience of myself. I experience my own ability to take risks through facilitating this event. I experience my terror at the moment where the unscripted and spontaneous event occurs. Our drama has afforded me the opportunity to fully experience my fear in the role of 'The Artist'. Yet I have also experienced my own ability to both embrace and move through that fear. When the need for spontaneous action occurs in my life beyond this enactment, I may find myself frozen and muted or I may find myself able to act. I have seen that there is more than one possibility. Additionally, I see through the enactment of 'Maria', the creative product, that I can be totally present in a moment and be taken care of: hence, not always the caretaker.

Everyone has got something. Everyone has offered something. This, I think, is the essence of nurturing.

When we are engaged in any creative process, we call upon technique, experience, and then we let everything go. I now understand that letting go is not an ability or learned skill. It is, necessarily, an unplanned, untimed, unexpected event. It is an accident.

My future stepped into me on the night of this enactment. I see myself as I am – both flawed and gifted. I feel both exposed and exhilarated by the process.
Robert Landy

Delayed in Delhi

In the temporary groups formed in our day-to-day lives, such as in a cinema or on an underground train, there is little or no communication between the people in the group. If, however, a train stops in a tunnel for a while, people will often start talking to each other, partly I think as reassurance that everything is all right, and to mask any nervousness they may be feeling. My own experience of this kind of situation was as the result of a delayed flight. We landed badly, damaging the plane on the first leg of our journey, and were forced to spend two nights in New Delhi waiting for a replacement.

Initially there seemed to be a general feeling of relief at our lucky escape from potential disaster. Then came confusion as everyone tried to find out what was going on. Would we have to stay in the airport? Where was our luggage? We were herded off to a hotel where we were informed it was too late for a meal, although we hadn't eaten for hours. Tiredness turned to indignation and some people, including myself and my partner, demanded that we be given something to eat. A small group of us began to form, united in our efforts to win this small battle, which we eventually did.

As time went by and information about our departure time was not forthcoming, our group of seven or eight people took it in turns singly or in small groups to badger the hotel management and airline to let us know what was going on. We all swapped room numbers and passed on any news to the others as we received it.

A self-appointed leader and spokesman emerged, a university professor older than the rest of us. He obviously felt that he was most capable of dealing with the situation, and took it upon himself to gather information and pass it on to everyone, and also let our grievances as a group be known to anyone who would listen to him.

Once we had become resigned to the fact that we were stranded in New Delhi, we took the opportunity to explore the city and enjoy ourselves. We all got to know each other quite well in a couple of days, and by the time we eventually touched down at Heathrow we had handed round our addresses to keep in touch. We then went our separate ways back to normal life, feeling like we had been playing parts in a disaster movie.

Cath Davis

Chapter 10

Evaluation

I believe that, when we work with any group, it is important not only to continually assess how people feel participating within the group, but also to let them evaluate the whole. Being able to write down how they feel is important for them and it is also important for the group leader because it helps the evaluation of what worked and what did not. Evaluation helps to keep a tab on progress, helps in the direction. It also offers some kind of guide for outsiders to see how a particular group went, particularly important when we are in receipt of some kind of grant funding.

It does not take long to evaluate and it really is worth doing. Evaluate at the end of a session or at the end of a run of sessions with the same group. Hand out the evaluation sheets and get people to fill them in and hand them back to you before they go. If you let people take them home to fill in and return to you, not only will people forget some of the workshop but you will probably find that over half the participants won't even remember to return the evaluation sheet.

The following sample evaluation sheet may be photocopied or used as a basis for one of your own.

Workshop evaluation

Please spend 10 minutes filling in this sheet. We need this feedback to ensure that your needs are met and to improve future workshops.

Name *(optional)* _____ Date _____

Address *(optional)* _____

_____

Please state in what capacity you attended

School/group name _____

Type of workshop _____

Your overall impression of the workshop was (please tick ☐):
☐ excellent ☐ good ☐ fair ☐ poor

The practical value of the workshop to you was (please tick ☐):
☐ excellent ☐ good ☐ fair ☐ poor

What was the most successful feature of the workshop?

_____

What was the least successful feature of the workshop?

_____

If you could change one thing about the workshop, what would it be?

_____

Do you think that more or less time should have been spent on any section?

_____

Were there any areas which you wanted to find out about that weren't included in the workshop?

_____

Please comment on the tutor(s)' effectiveness and presentation

_____

_____

Overall, did this workshop reach your expectations? Yes/No.
If not, can you say why?

_____

_____

Last words

I hope that you have been able to get something out of this manual, that it has answered some of your questions, given you some new ideas or stimulated new ways of working.

A group of people co-operating can achieve much. Separated from the group, we can become isolated individuals. Some people today suggest that there is no such thing as *society*, only *individuals*. I believe that as isolated individuals we lose many of our strengths, such as our ability to share with each other: to share ideas, stories, possibilities, pathways, direction, resources, emotions and the concept of what is right and wrong, to name but a few.

Some cultures find the western need for isolation ('An Englishman's home is his castle') very strange. For the Temiars of Malaysia, hiding away in a house for any length of time would seem nonsensical, unless one was ill. Working in the city, I do need my own space now and again, but I also need other people. We need other people to help us develop as individuals and as cultural and spiritual beings. We need other people to help us develop our professional identity and we need other people to help us find solutions to difficulties. And remember, working with people can be great fun: groupwork can be great fun.

I would like to end with a word of caution. Group leaders often hold a lot of power. It is important to remember *never to abuse this power*.

Useful addresses

There are groups that explore and celebrate almost every human need and desire. The list is endless and I have therefore not attempted to cover everything. The following list provides a wide range of groups, perhaps including that elusive group you have been seeking. Button & Bloom (1992) provide an excellent resource book, with many contact names and addresses. If you still have difficulty in finding what you want, remember that your local library (or the Internet) is probably your best resource.

African Roots Dance and Theatre
Yolande Burke
48 Newham Green
Green Lanes
London N16
United Kingdom

Age Exchange
The Reminiscence Centre
11 Blackheath Village
London SE3 9LA
United Kingdom

American Society of Group Psychotherapy and Psychodrama
301 N. Harrison Street
Suite 508
Princeton, New Jersey 08540
USA

Association for Dance Movement Therapy
99 South Hill Park
London NW3 2SP

Association of Humanistic Psychology
Box BCM AHPP
London WC1N 3XX
United Kingdom

Augusto Boal
(Theatre of the Oppressed)
Centro Do Teatro Do Oprimido
Do Rio De Janeiro
Rue Francisco Otaviano 185
Apt 41 CEP 22.080-040 Ipanema
Arpoador, Brasil

British Association for Music Therapy
69 Avondale Avenue
East Barnet
Hertfordshire EN4 8NB
United Kingdom

British Association of Art Therapies
11a Richmond Road
Brighton BN2 3RL
United Kingdom

British Homeopathic Society
27a Devonshire Street
London W1N 1RJ
United Kingdom

Centre for Stress Management
156 Westcombe Hill
Blackheath
London SE3 7DH
United Kingdom

Charter 88 (Violations of rights)
Exmouth House
3–11 Pine Street
London EC1R 0JH
United Kingdom

Childline
Freepost 1111
London N1 0BR
United Kingdom

CRUSE Bereavement Care
Cruse House
126 Sheen Road
Richmond
London TW9 1UR
United Kingdom

**Eagle Wing Centre for
Contemporary Shamanism**
58 Westbere Road
London NW2 3RU
United Kingdom

Eating Disorders Association
Sackville Place
44 Magdalen Street
Norwich NR3 1JE
United Kingdom

Everyman
PO Box 49
Oxford OX2 2YH
United Kingdom

Findhorn Foundation
(New Age practices)
The Park
Findhorn Bay
Morays IV36 0TZ
United Kingdom

**Gender Dysphoria Trust
International**
BM Box 7624
London WC1N 3XX
United Kingdom

Graeae Theatre Company
Interchange Studios
Dalby Street
London NW5 3NQ
United Kingdom

Holistic Aromatherapy
108b Haverstock Hill
London NW3 2BD
United Kingdom

Independent Theatre Council
12 The Leather Market
Weston Street
London SE1 3ER
United Kingdom

Institute of Group Analysis
1 Daleham Gardens
London NW3 5BY
United Kingdom

Institute of Psych-Analysis
63 Cavendish Street
London W1H 7RD
United Kingdom

Institute of Rational–Emotive Therapy
14 Winchester Avenue
London NW6 7TU
United Kingdom

LARRIE (Race relations)
35 Great Smith Street
London SW1P 3BJ
United Kingdom

Mobility International
rue de Manchester
B-1070 Brussels
Belgium

Moreno Institute
(Psychodrama)
259 Wolcott Avenue
Beacon
New York 12508
USA

National Association of Citizens' Advice Bureaux
115 Pentonville Road
London N1 9LZ
United Kingdom

National Council for Voluntary Organisations
26 Bedford Square
London WC1B 3HU
United Kingdom

RADAR (Disability)
25 Mortimer Street
London W1N 8AB
United Kingdom

Relate (Marriage guidance)
Herbert Gray College
Little Church Street
Rugby CV21 3AP
United Kingdom

Samye Ling
Eskdalemuir
Langholm
Dumfriesshire DG13 0QL
United Kingdom

Sarah Argent
(Children's Theatre Association)
APTCHYP
Unicorn Arts Theatre
Great Newport Street
London WC2H 7JB
United Kingdom

Saros Foundation (Occult)
121 Hollybush Lane
Hampton
Middlesex
TW12 2QY
United Kingdom

Sesame
The Central School of Speech and Drama
Embassy Theatre
Eton Avenue
London NW3 3HY
United Kingdom

Sivananda Yoga Vedanta Centre
51 Foulsham Road
London SW15 1AZ
United Kingdom

SPOD (Disability)
286 Camden Road
London N7 0BJ
United Kingdom

TACADE (Drug addiction)
3rd Floor
Furness House
Trafford Road
Salford M5 2XJ
United Kingdom

The Dream Research Centre
8 Willow Road
London NW3
United Kingdom

The Gestalt Centre
64 Warwick Road
St Albans AL1 4DL
United Kingdom

**The Institute of
Dramatherapy at
Roehampton**
Faculty of Arts and Humanities
The Roehampton Institute
Digby Stuart College
Roehampton Lane
London SW15 5PH
United Kingdom

**The Matriarchy Research
and Reclaim Group**
Cloverly House
Erwood
Builth Wells
Powys LD2 3EZ
United Kingdom

**The National College of
Hypnosis and Psychotherapy**
12 Cross Street
Nelson
Lancashire BB9 7EN
United Kingdom

**The UK Standing Conference
for Psychotherapy**
167 Sumatra Road
London NW6 1PN
United Kingdom

The Women's Therapy Centre
6 Manor Gardens
London N7 6LA
United Kingdom

The Vegetarian Society
Parkdale
Dunham Road
Altrincham
Cheshire WA14 4QG
United Kingdom

Tie Tours
(Theatre of the Oppressed
and problem solving)
99 Southfleet
Malden Road
London NW5 4DH
United Kingdom

Bibliography

Adland DE, *The Group Approach to Drama*, Longmans, London, 1964.

Aveline M & Dryden W (eds), *Group Therapy in Britain*, Open University Press, Milton Keynes, 1988.

Bales RF, *Interaction Process Analysis: A Method for the Study of Small Groups*, Addison-Wesley, New York, 1950.

Bandler B & Grinder J, *Frogs into Princes*, Eden Grove Editions, London, 1990.

Barker C, *Theatre Games*, Methuen, London, 1977.

Baumslag B & Chandler B, *Theory and Problems of Group Theory*, McGraw-Hill, New York, 1968.

Berger J, *Ways of Seeing*, Penguin, London, 1972.

Berne E, *The Structure and Dynamics of Organisations and Groups*, Grove Press, New York, 1963.

Berne E, *Games People Play*, Penguin, Harmondsworth, 1964.

Berry C, *Your Voice and How to Use it Successfully*, Harrap, London, 1975.

Boal A, *Theatre of the Oppressed*, Pluto Press, New York, 1988.

Boal A, *Games for Actors and Non-Actors*, Routledge, London, 1992.

Boal A, *The Rainbow of Desire*, Routledge, London, 1995.

Bonner H, *Group Dynamics: Principles and Applications*, Ronald Press, New York, 1959.

Brandes D & Philips H, *Gamesters' Handbook*, Stanley Thornes, Cheltenham, 1977.

Brearley G & Birchley P, *Introducing Counselling Skills and Techniques*, Wolf Publishing, London, 1992.

Brook P, *The Empty Space*, Penguin, London, 1968.

Button J & Bloom W (eds), *The Seekers Guide*, Aquarian/Thorsons, London, 1992.

Campbell J, *Creative Art in Groupwork*, Winslow Press, Bicester, 1993.

Cartledge G & Milburn JF, *Teaching Social Skills to Children*, p100, Pergamon Press, Elmsford, NY, 1981.

Cattanach A, *Drama for People with Special Needs*, A & C Black, London, 1992.

Chesner A, *Dramatherapy for People with Learning Disabilities*, Jessica Kingsley, London, 1995.

Christen L, *Drama Skills for Life*, Currency Press, Sydney, 1992.

Clark B, *Group Theatre*, Pitman Publishing, London, 1971.

Coppet de D, *Understanding Rituals*, Routledge, London, 1992.

Cox J (ed), *Transcultural Psychiatry*, Croom Helm, London, 1986.

Dayton T, *Drama Games*, Innerlook Inc, Florida, 1990.

Douglas T, *Groupwork Practice*, Tavistock/Routlege, London, 1976.

Douglas T, *Groups*, Routledge, London, 1991.

Dynes R, *Creative Writing in Groupwork*, Winslow Press, Bicester, 1988.

Dynes R, *Creative Games in Groupwork*, Winslow Press, Bicester, 1990.

Fagan J & Shepherd L (eds), *Gestalt Therapy Now*, Penguin Books, Harmondsworth, 1972.

Foster R, *Knowing in My Bones*, Adam and Charles Black, London, 1976.

Foulks SH, *Introduction to Group-Analytic Psychotherapy*, Maresfield Reprints, London, 1983.

Fox J (ed), *The Essential Moreno*, Springer, New York, 1987.

Gelb M, *Body Learning*, Aurum Press, London, 1981.

Gersie A, *Earthtales*, Green Print, London, 1992.

Grotowski J, *Towards a Poor Theatre*, Methuen, London, 1969.

Hewitt J, *Meditation*, Hodder & Stoughton, London, 1978.

Hickson A, *Workshop Resource Pack*, Tie Tours, London, 1994.

Hickson A, *Creative Action Methods in Groupwork*, Winslow Press, Bicester, 1995.

Hinshelwood RD, *What Happens in Groups*, Free Association Books, London, 1987.

Holmes P, Karp M & Watson M (eds), *Psychodrama Since Moreno*, Routledge, London, 1994.

Houston G, *The Red Book of Groups*, Houston, London, 1987.

Jennings S, *Remedial Drama*, A & C Black, London, 1978.

Jennings S, *Creative Drama in Groupwork*, Winslow Press, Bicester, 1986.

Jennings S, *Dramatherapy Theory and Practice*, Vol 1, Routledge, London, 1987.

Jennings S, *Dramatherapy with Families, Groups and Individuals*, Jessica Kingsley, London, 1987.

Jennings S, *Dramatherapy Theory and Practice*, Vol 2, Routledge, London, 1992.

Jennings S & Minde A, *Art Therapy and Dramatherapy*, Jessica Kingsley, London, 1993.

Jennings S, Cattanach A, Mitchell S, Chesner A & Meldrum B, *The Handbook of Dramatherapy*, Routledge, London, 1994.

Johnston K, *Impro*, Methuen, London, 1979.

Kirsta A, *Stress Survival*, Gala, London, 1989.

Kovel J, *A Complete Guide to Therapy*, Harvesters Press, Brighton, 1976.

Kumiega J, *The Theatre of Grotowski*, Methuen, London, 1985.

Littlewood R & Lipsedge M, *Aliens and Alienists*, Penguin, London, 1982.

Long S, *A Structural Analysis of Small Groups*, Routledge, London, 1993.

Maré PB de, *Perspectives in Group Psychotherapy*, George Allen & Unwin, London, 1972.

McCallion M, *The Voice Book*, Faber & Faber, London, 1988.

Midgley M, *Beast & Man*, Methuen, London, 1978.

Moreno JD *et al*, *Group Psychotherapy and Psychodrama*, Volume XXVII, No. 1–4, Beacon House Inc, New York, 1974.

Murphy RC, *Psychotherapy Based on Human Longing*, Pendle Hill Leaflets, London, 1960.

Parsons T, Shils E & Olds J, *Values, Motives and Systems of Action*, Harvard University Press, Cambridge, Mass., 1951.

Perls F, *The Gestalt Approach*, Bantam Books, New York, 1973.

Smith P, *Group Processes*, Penguin, London, 1970.

Spolin V, *Theatre Games for Rehearsal*, Northwestern University Press, Evanston, 1985.

Stewart KR, 'Magico-religious beliefs and practices in primitive society – a sociological interpretation of their therapeutic aspects', Doctoral thesis, London School of Economics, 1947.

Storr A, *The Art of Psychotherapy*, Routledge, New York, 1980.

Weber A, *Introduction to Psychology*, Harper Collins, London, 1991.

Winn L, *Post Traumatic Stress Disorder and Dramatherapy*, Jessica Kingsley, London, 1994.

Index to activities